Current
CONTROVERSIES

| Iran

DISCARD

Other Books in the Current Controversies Series

Iran

Debra A. Miller, Book Editor

GREENHAVEN PRESS
A part of Gale, Cengage Learning

Detroit • New York • San Francisco • New Haven, Conn • Waterville, Maine • London

Christine Nasso, *Publisher*
Elizabeth Des Chenes, *Managing Editor*

© 2011 Greenhaven Press, a part of Gale, Cengage Learning

Gale and Greenhaven Press are registered trademarks used herein under license.

For more information, contact:
Greenhaven Press
27500 Drake Rd.
Farmington Hills, MI 48331-3535
Or you can visit our Internet site at gale.cengage.com

For product information and technology assistance, contact us at

Gale Customer Support, 1-800-877-4253
For permission to use material from this text or product, submit all requests online at www.cengage.com/permissions

Further permissions questions can be emailed to permissionrequest@cengage.com

Articles in Greenhaven Press anthologies are often edited for length to meet page requirements. In addition, original titles of these works are changed to clearly present the main thesis and to explicitly indicate the author's opinion. Every effort is made to ensure that Greenhaven Press accurately reflects the original intent of the authors. Every effort has been made to trace the owners of copyrighted material.

Cover image © Liang Youchang/XinHua/Xinhua Press/Corbis.

LIBRARY OF CONGRESS CATALOGING-IN-PUBLICATION DATA

Iran / Debra A. Miller, book editor.
    p. cm. -- (Current controversies)
    Includes bibliographical references and index.
    ISBN 978-0-7377-5181-9 (hardcover) -- ISBN 978-0-7377-5182-6 (pbk.)
    1. Iran--Juvenile literature. 2. Iran--Politics and government--1997--Juvenile literature. 3. Iran--Foreign relations--1997---Juvenile literature. 4. Iran--Foreign relations--United States--Juvenile literature. 5. United States--Foreign relations--Iran--Juvenile literature. I. Miller, Debra A.
    DS318.9.I7254 2010
    955.06'1--dc22

                                                                    2010024430

Printed in the United States of America
1 2 3 4 5 6 7 14 13 12 11 10

Contents

No: Iran's Nuclear Program Is Not Peaceful

Chapter 2: Does Iran Want to Dominate Iraq?

Chapter 3: Will the Iranian Green Revolution Succeed?

Chapter 4: What Approach Should the United States Take Toward Iran?

Iran has been defying international demands that it stop enriching uranium, and since Iran has failed to respond to diplomatic initiatives, it is time to turn to tough sanctions. If U.S. officials cannot convince the United Nations Security Council to vote for sanctions, the United States should pursue other avenues, such as forming a coalition with Europe, seeking support for international economic boycotts, or enforcing the 1996 Iran Sanctions Act to penalize companies doing business with Iran's energy sector.

Foreword

By definition, controversies are "discussions of questions in which opposing opinions clash" (Webster's Twentieth Century Dictionary Unabridged). Few would deny that controversies are a pervasive part of the human condition and exist on virtually every level of human enterprise. Controversies transpire between individuals and among groups, within nations and between nations. Controversies supply the grist necessary for progress by providing challenges and challengers to the status quo. They also create atmospheres where strife and warfare can flourish. A world without controversies would be a peaceful world; but it also would be, by and large, static and prosaic.

The Series' Purpose

The purpose of the Current Controversies series is to explore many of the social, political, and economic controversies dominating the national and international scenes today. Titles selected for inclusion in the series are highly focused and specific. For example, from the larger category of criminal justice, Current Controversies deals with specific topics such as police brutality, gun control, white collar crime, and others. The debates in Current Controversies also are presented in a useful, timeless fashion. Articles and book excerpts included in each title are selected if they contribute valuable, long-range ideas to the overall debate. And wherever possible, current information is enhanced with historical documents and other relevant materials. Thus, while individual titles are current in focus, every effort is made to ensure that they will not become quickly outdated. Books in the Current Controversies series will remain important resources for librarians, teachers, and students for many years.

In addition to keeping the titles focused and specific, great care is taken in the editorial format of each book in the series. Book introductions and chapter prefaces are offered to provide background material for readers. Chapters are organized around several key questions that are answered with diverse opinions representing all points on the political spectrum. Materials in each chapter include opinions in which authors clearly disagree as well as alternative opinions in which authors may agree on a broader issue but disagree on the possible solutions. In this way, the content of each volume in Current Controversies mirrors the mosaic of opinions encountered in society. Readers will quickly realize that there are many viable answers to these complex issues. By questioning each author's conclusions, students and casual readers can begin to develop the critical thinking skills so important to evaluating opinionated material.

Current Controversies is also ideal for controlled research. Each anthology in the series is composed of primary sources taken from a wide gamut of informational categories including periodicals, newspapers, books, U.S. and foreign government documents, and the publications of private and public organizations. Readers will find factual support for reports, debates, and research papers covering all areas of important issues. In addition, an annotated table of contents, an index, a book and periodical bibliography, and a list of organizations to contact are included in each book to expedite further research.

Perhaps more than ever before in history, people are confronted with diverse and contradictory information. During the Persian Gulf War, for example, the public was not only treated to minute-to-minute coverage of the war, it was also inundated with critiques of the coverage and countless analyses of the factors motivating U.S. involvement. Being able to sort through the plethora of opinions accompanying today's major issues, and to draw one's own conclusions, can be a complicated and frustrating struggle. It is the editors' hope that Current Controversies will help readers with this struggle.

Introduction

The Iranian Revolution, also called the Islamic Revolution, was a political uprising in Iran in 1979 that overthrew Iran's secular monarchy government led by a king, Mohammad Reza Shah Pahlavi, and replaced it with an Islamic republic—basically a theocracy, or government ruled by religious laws—under the control of Ayatollah Ruhollah Khomeini, a popular religious leader. The revolution was, in large part, an ultraconservative rejection of the shah's decades-long effort to marginalize the role of Islamic clerics and the religion of Islam in the country's legal and social systems, as well as his dictatorial and often repressive style of governing. It also was a reaction to the shah's strong ties to the Western world and culture, particularly that of the United States, which many Iranians viewed as offensive and overbearing.

The shah began his reign as king of Iran in 1941, when his father abdicated the throne. After World War II, following a crisis that caused him to flee Iran, the shah returned to the throne and initiated a program to modernize Iran, which he saw as a backward and underdeveloped country. With significant help from the United States, Iran implemented various economic development projects including new steel mills, oil refineries, aluminum smelters, machine tool factories, automobile manufacturers, and plans to build a series of nuclear power plants. Iran's economy grew rapidly, increasing prosperity for many Iranians. Iran's new wealth, in turn, enabled the shah to dramatically improve public education and health services. The shah's reforms also included legal and social changes that increased the rights of women and transferred legal matters involving families from religious to secular courts.

Iran's educated classes mostly supported the shah's reforms, but the vast economic changes also brought some problems such as inflation, which hurt Iran's poorer classes. Many

Islamic religious leaders also bitterly opposed the shah's secular reforms and objected strongly to U.S. and Western influences in Iran. A leading conservative religious cleric, Ayatollah Ruhollah Khomeini, spoke out strongly against the shah, issuing a fatwa (religious edict) against the reforms in 1963 and encouraging people to protest the government changes. The shah responded by arresting Khomeini and expelling him into exile in the neighboring country of Iraq. The government then declared martial law and brutally crushed all dissent, killing thousands of rioters and demonstrators. In the years after the 1963 event, the shah, fearful of losing power, continued to censure and repress religious opposition in Iran, even as Khomeini unleashed verbal and written attacks on the shah from exile.

Protests against the shah's rule erupted again in 1978, when thousands of religious students took to the streets demanding restoration of religious freedoms. The Iranian police, on orders from the shah to crush the uprising, shot into the crowd and killed a number of demonstrators. The government's violence only helped to ensure that the demonstrations continued. Over ensuing months, religious clerics joined the demonstrations; Khomeini called for the shah's overthrow; and religious students and sympathizers attacked liquor stores, movie theaters, and other establishments that they considered to be offensive to Islam. Realizing the danger to his rule, the shah sought to mollify the opposition by making various changes, but it was simply too late. The size of the demonstrations grew steadily, and security forces eventually were overwhelmed. The shah left Iran for exile in January 1979, and two weeks later Ayatollah Khomeini returned to Iran as a conquering hero. On April 1, 1979, Iran voted by national referendum to become an Islamic republic and Khomeini became supreme leader a few months later.

Khomeini instituted a government that was directly ruled by Islamic law, called sharia. In accordance with the ultraconscrvative teachings of sharia, Khomeini quickly changed many of the rules of social conduct in Iran. He declared, for example, that females could not be judges; that women had to wear the hijab religious head covering; that alcohol, gambling, and nightclubs were banned; and that men and women had to be segregated in public places such as buses and schools. Khomeini also required that all persons running the government, the military, the judiciary, businesses, and schools and universities support and abide by Islamic rule. Former friends and supporters of the shah who were unable to escape from Iran were arrested, given show trials, and summarily executed. Newspapers, films, and other media were banned and the government nationalized, or took over, the nation's banks and major industries. In addition, Khomeini was openly hostile toward the United States; and in November 1979, he allowed his followers to seize the American embassy in Iran and hold fifty-three American diplomats as hostages. Iran proposed to set the hostages free if the United States forced the shah to return to Iran, but the United States refused and the hostages were not released until January 1981, after the shah had died of cancer.

Although Khomeini died in 1989, he was succeeded by a new supreme leader, Ayatollah Ali Khamenei. Under Iran's complicated Islamic political system, the supreme leader is chosen by a group of clerical experts who are elected by the people every eight years. The supreme leader retains most of the political power in Iran. He appoints members to Iran's governing institutions (such as the Guardian Council and the Expediency Council), picks the head of the judiciary, controls the armed forces, and makes all major decisions on security, defense, and foreign policy. Yet Iran also has a president and parliament elected by the people and charged with running the country. A conservative former mayor of Tehran (Iran's capital), Mahmoud Ahmadinejad was elected Iran's president in 2005, and Iran's parliament is also controlled by conservative Islamists.

Under Islamic rule, Iran has remained openly hostile to America and has supported the spread of radical Islam in countries throughout the region. In terms of U.S. foreign policy, the country is viewed as a potential problem for several reasons. Many foreign policy experts believe the nation has provided support for terrorist activities and that it seeks to acquire nuclear weapons that could be used to attack Israel or even the United States. According to many observers, Iran also has sought to exert its influence in Iraq, which is struggling to stabilize after a U.S.-led invasion and war that toppled the dictatorship of Iraqi president Saddam Hussein. Additionally, in 2009, Iran's own political stability was upset by widespread demonstrations by Iranian youths objecting to what were viewed as fraudulent presidential elections and demanding new elections, greater personal freedoms, and more democracy. The authors of the viewpoints in *Current Controversies: Iran* debate various issues facing modern Iran, including whether Iran's nuclear program is peaceful, whether Iran wants to dominate Iraq, whether Iran's protest movement (called the Green Revolution or Green Movement) will succeed, and what approach the United States should take in dealing with Iran.

CHAPTER 1

Is Iran's Nuclear Program Peaceful?

Chapter Preface

Iran's current interest in nuclear technology is not new; it began decades ago during the reign of Iran's late king, Mohammad Reza Shah Pahlavi, with the encouragement of the United States. In 1957, as part of U.S. President Dwight D. Eisenhower's Atoms for Peace campaign, the United States agreed to provide nuclear fuel, equipment, and other assistance to help Iran develop nuclear capability for peaceful uses such as electricity, health care, and medicine. Iran's first nuclear facility, the Tehran Nuclear Research Center, was built in 1967 at Tehran University and housed a research reactor supplied by the United States. On July 1, 1968, Iran signed the Nuclear Non-Proliferation Treaty (NPT), also known as the Treaty on the Non-Proliferation of Nuclear Weapons, an international treaty designed to limit the spread of nuclear weapons based on three pillars: nonproliferation, disarmament, and peaceful use. Iran, therefore, retained the right under the NPT to research and develop nuclear power for the production of electricity and other peaceful purposes.

With the help of the United States as well as other countries such as France and Germany, Iran's nuclear program grew substantially during the 1970s. During this period, wars and oil embargoes in the Middle East caused concerns about possible future fossil fuel energy shortages and led the shah to embark on a plan to increase Iran's nuclear power production. As part of this plan, in 1974, Iran established the Atomic Energy Organization of Iran and announced that it would soon produce twenty-three thousand megawatts of electricity from nuclear power. Iran also signed contracts with companies in France and Germany, and was negotiating with the United States, to construct new nuclear plants and provide nuclear fuel.

Western support for Iran's nuclear program, however, began to erode in the late 1970s as the shah's power weakened and Iran's government became less stable. The close relationship between Iran and the United States disappeared completely in February 1979, when the Islamic Revolution overthrew the shah's pro-Western government and replaced it with an anti-American, Islamic republic led by Ayatollah Ruhollah Khomeini, an Islamic religious leader. The withdrawal of U.S. and Western aid after the Islamic Revolution slowed the growth of Iran's nuclear program significantly. In addition, many Iranian nuclear scientists fled Iran; Khomeini appeared to have religious objections to nuclear weapons; and Israel, fearful that the new regime would pose a threat, bombed Iran's only existing nuclear facility in 1981.

Most observers date the rebirth of Iran's nuclear program with the death of Khomeini in 1989. His successor, Ayatollah Ali Khamenei, began an effort to once again boost the country's nuclear research, build new reactors, and acquire nuclear fuel with the help of new allies—Russia, China, Pakistan, and North Korea. Iran also is working to produce its own fuel and, according to reports, has built a vast network of uranium mines, enrichment plants, and other facilities to advance this goal.

Although Iran continues to maintain that its intent is to develop peaceful nuclear power, many foreign policy experts fear that the regime may be seeking to build nuclear weapons. These fears have been fueled, in large part, by what many people see as Iran's concealment of its nuclear program. In 2002 and 2003, for example, the world learned that Iran had built two facilities—a heavy-water production plant and two enrichment facilities—in secret. Most recently, in February 2008, intelligence collected by the United States revealed that Iran has been pursuing a secret uranium-processing program, high-explosives testing, and reentry vehicle designs—all actions that suggest the country's end goal might be nuclear weapons.

The fears about Iran's nuclear ambitions have led the United States and the European Union to impose unilateral economic sanctions on Iran. In addition, the United Nations (UN) Security Council (the organization's governing body) has passed a series of resolutions imposing economic, financial, and travel sanctions to punish Iran for continued uranium enrichment and to prevent the sale or transfer of sensitive nuclear technology. U.S. President Barack Obama's call for a fourth round of UN economic sanctions against Iran was approved in early June 2010, with Turkey and Brazil voting against the measure. Meanwhile, since no incontrovertible evidence of nuclear weapons has been found, the debate about Iran's nuclear intentions continues. This chapter focuses on this fundamental question—whether Iran's nuclear program is peaceful or designed to produce nuclear weapons.

Iran Needs Nuclear Power for Peaceful Purposes

Habib Siddiqui

Habib Siddiqui is a Muslim peace and human rights activist. He is an author from Bangladesh, who lives in the United States and has written and blogged extensively about global politics and human rights.

The relationship between the governments of Iran and the USA has been tense and nasty since the fall of the Shah [Iran's former king, who was overthrown in 1979]. During the long Iran-Iraq War, the USA and her allies even supported the Iraqi regime when it invaded Iran. On July 3, 1988, the U.S. Navy's guided missile cruiser USS *Vincennes* shot down Iran Air Flight 655 (IR655) killing all 290 passengers and crew aboard, including 66 children. It was the highest death toll of any aviation incident in the Indian Ocean and the highest death toll of any incident involving an Airbus A300 anywhere in the world. At the time of the attack, *Vincennes*, fitted with the then-new Aegis combat system, was traversing the Strait of Hormuz inside Iranian territorial waters, and the IR655 was within Iranian airspace. Worse still, after completing their tour, the *Vincennes* crew was awarded Combat Action Ribbons for having actively participated in ground or surface combat and its captain, William C. Rogers III, received the Legion of Merit.

Iran's Relationship with the United States After 9/11

Then came 9/11 [September 11, 2001, terrorist attacks on the United States], which Iran's supreme leader Ayatollah Ali Khamenei condemned. Thousands of ordinary Iranians held

Habib Siddiqui, "Western Meddling with Iran's Nuclear Program Is Unacceptable," Drhabibsiddiqui.blogspot.com, February 4, 2010. Reproduced by permission of the author.

candles during vigils in Tehran to mourn the loss of life in the United States. President Mohammad Khatami set the tone for Iran's reaction with a statement that in Persian rang with deep compassion: "On behalf of the Iranian people and the Islamic Republic, I denounce the terrorist measures, which led to the killing of defenseless people, and I express my deep sorrow and sympathy with the American people."

[The United States and Israel] want Iran to be disarmed the same way Iraq was seven years ago.

Then followed January 29, 2002, when President GW [George W.] Bush in his State of the Union speech claimed Iran as part of an "axis of evil." From that moment onward, there was hardly anything positive to build bridges between the two countries. Iraq, the other Middle Eastern country belonging to Bush's evil axis, has already been invaded and occupied in 2003 under the pretext of possessing the WMDs [weapons of mass destruction], which were never to be found. The Anglo-American invasion was itself declared illegal by no less of a figure than the secretary-general of the UN [United Nations]. Saddam Hussein [Iraq's president] was subsequently hanged. But who cares or dares to put Bush and [former British prime minister Tony] Blair in the electric chair for their genocidal campaign in Iraq that killed thousands of Anglo-American soldiers and hundreds of thousands of unarmed Iraqi civilians, and destroyed the entire infrastructure of the country?

Iran remains intact, more than eight years after Bush's evil declaration, much to the chagrin of Israel and her Amen Corner inside the Capitol Hill of the USA. They want Iran to be disarmed the same way Iraq was seven years ago so that there won't be anyone left in the already emasculated Middle East to threaten or challenge the existence of the state of Israel.

They claim Iran is developing nuclear weapons, which are, as they claim, existential threats to the only nuclear power in the Middle East. How wonderful!

Iran's Nuclear Program

There is no doubt that Iran has a nuclear program. It is actually 51 years old, dating back to 1959 when Iran purchased a research reactor from the USA. Mohammad Reza Shah [Pahlavi], a trusted friend of the USA and Israel who was installed into power in a CIA [Central Intelligence Agency] coup that overthrew a democratically elected government, had a grandiose plan to build 23 nuclear power reactors by the 1990s. The USA and the Western world had no problem with the Shah's ambitious project. And yet Iran's current plans to construct seven nuclear power plants by 2025 to meet growing energy demand are considered too ambitious and unacceptable by the same countries. They question: Why should Iran go nuclear when she has the third largest reservoir of oil and gas? Forgotten in this context are the facts that Iran does not have enough refining capacity to process her own crude oil (forcing her to import refined oil from outside) and that when all the developed countries around the world are going nuclear or making serious efforts to go carbon-free, away from fossil fuel–based technology, why should Iran, a country with enormous talented human resources and a rich history of non-aggression, remain behind in technology evolution?

Iran is neither Somalia nor Haiti. Her leaders have repeatedly assured the world that their nuclear program has nothing to do with weapons, which are considered haram [forbidden by Islamic law] by its Islamic clerics. Iran's President Dr. [Mahmoud] Ahmadinejad declared, "We believe that the possession of nuclear bombs is immoral." The Iranian government has for long demanded a nuclear-free world, let alone the Middle East. The International Atomic Energy Agency (IAEA) inspectors have not found any evidence of weapons programs either inside Iran. On September 2, 2009, its outgoing director general Dr. [Mohamed] ElBaradei said that Iran was not going to produce a nuclear weapon in the near future and the threat posed had been exaggerated. Unlike Israel, North Korea, India and Pakistan, Iran is actually a signatory to the Nuclear Non-Proliferation Treaty (NPT) [Treaty on the Non-Proliferation of Nuclear Weapons] and submitting itself to the jurisdiction of the IAEA. And yet it seems kosher for the nuclear Brahmin states to disallow Iran's legitimate aspirations for nuclear power.

Israel and her Western patrons are suspicious about Iran's uranium enrichment program, suspecting that the enriched fuel could be used for the weapons program. However, the enrichment level of 3.5 percent, achieved thus far by Iranian scientists, remains far below what is necessary (90 percent) for highly enriched uranium or weapon-grade plutonium. Iran has a reactor in Tehran that produces nuclear medicine (20 different kinds thus far), based on radioactive technologies. She requires 19.75 percent enrichment to foresee her needs for the next two decades. Iran, being far short of producing that target, has been buying this material from other countries. According to President Ahmadinejad, Iran is even willing to purchase this material from the USA.

[Iran's] leaders have repeatedly assured the world that their nuclear program has nothing to do with weapons, which are considered haram [forbidden by Islamic law] by its Islamic clerics.

Israel's Nuclear Program and the Threat to Iran

What is so bizarre in this nuclear debate with Iran is that the USA has no problem rewarding a country like India, which has not signed the NPT. The Obama administration renewed previous Bush commitment and signed a bilateral treaty with India last July [2009] for the construction of two U.S. civilian nuclear power reactors in India, which officials estimate could be worth about $10 billion to American companies.

From published reports it seems Israel has already chalked out a plan, under NATO [North Atlantic Treaty Organization, an alliance of sixteen countries] protection, to knock out Iran's suspected nuclear facilities. As we have already seen with Iraq, Mossad [an Israeli intelligence agency] agents are active inside Iran in killing Iranian scientists that are affiliated with the state-run nuclear research facilities. Not to be left behind, some Iranian traitors, affiliated with the terrorist group MKO [People's Mujahedin of Iran] and the deposed Shah's son (who lives in the USA), are trying to follow the footsteps of Ahmed Chalabi (of Iraq) to manufacture a pre-invasion Iraq-like environment for overthrow of the current Iranian regime, tainted by accusations of fraud in the last presidential election.

As noted by keen observers and area experts, Israel and her Jewish friends outside remain the most vociferous opponents of Iran's nuclear program. In recent months, Israeli leaders, all war criminals by any definition, are touring the world preaching for nuclear-free Iran. As noted earlier, the Zionist state wants to remain unchallenged in the region while undermining and denying legitimate aspirations of other countries in the region for nuclear energy for peaceful purpose. With the powerful Israel lobby active inside the USA and Europe, she has little to feel guilty of her criminal actions and illogical demands.

Fortunately, not everyone is fooled by Israel's devious ploys. Last September while attending the 64th session of the UN General Assembly and following his meeting with his Iranian counterpart Mahmoud Ahmadinejad, Brazilian President Luiz Inácio Lula da Silva said Iran was entitled to the same rights as any other country in its use of nuclear energy for peaceful purposes. "I defend for Iran the same rights with respect to nuclear energy that I do for Brazil," Lula told reporters outside the United Nations General Assembly. "If anyone is ashamed of having relations with Iran, it's not Brazil," he added.

In September 2009 the General Conference of the IAEA passed a landmark resolution urging Israel to open its entire nuclear program to IAEA inspection and join the NPT. The IAEA resolution had likewise warned of 'Israeli nuclear capabilities.' Egyptian Foreign Minister Ahmed Aboul Gheit, in a letter to all 15 members of the United Nations Security Council (UNSC), asked the council to enforce the observation. Aboul Gheit mentioned that Tel Aviv has been refusing to sign the nuclear NPT, adding that "Israel's nuclear capabilities cannot evade world attention." Egypt and other members of the Arab League [League of Arab States] upheld the decision which had been fiercely opposed by the US and its Western allies. Aboul Gheit also urged the UNSC to develop a time frame for a nuclear-free Middle East.

It is worth noting here that since 1958, when it began building its Dimona plutonium and uranium processing facility, Israel has reportedly manufactured hundreds of nuclear warheads earning a reputation as the sole owner of such hardware in the Middle East. Former US president Jimmy Carter, aerial footage and decades of recurrent reporting have attested to the existence of the armament. However, as is glaringly obvious, the Western countries, including the USA, are willing to overlook Israeli nuclear buildups in the region. Such a biased, hypocritical and criminal attitude does not allow any concerned person to hope for an easing of the tension in the Middle East.

Iran Is Not Capable of Making Nuclear Weapons in the Near Future

Muhammad Sahimi

Muhammad Sahimi is a professor of chemical engineering and materials science and a political columnist for Tehran Bureau, an independent news organization. He has been writing about Iran's nuclear program and its internal developments for several years.

Iran's announcement that it is going to produce enriched uranium at 19.75 percent, using its current stockpile of 3.5 percent low-enriched uranium (LEU), which it needs as fuel for the Tehran [Iran's capital city] research reactor (TRR) that produces medical isotopes, has stirred unwarranted war hysteria in the West. The International Atomic Energy Agency (IAEA) has confirmed that Iran will begin the enrichment at a level "less than 20 percent."

Note that the language of the IAEA statement and the 19.75 percent that Iran has set as the level of enrichment are both important, because any uranium enriched above 20 percent is considered to be high-enriched, normally associated with a nuclear bomb or device, even though in reality 90 percent enrichment is necessary for a nuclear weapon. So, just try to imagine if the IAEA discovers traces of uranium in Iran enriched at 20.1 percent. The world would be bombarded with the news that Iran has produced high-enriched uranium suitable for nuclear weapons!

Iran's Plans

Iran plans to begin testing the enrichment process using the Natanz Pilot Fuel Enrichment Plant (PFEP), which is a small-scale facility used previously for centrifuge research, development, and testing. The PFEP can hold six centrifuge cascades, each with 164 centrifuges, but only three or four have actually been installed. According to Reuters [an international news service], Iran has begun introducing its 3.5 percent LEU at the Natanz PFEP under the IAEA supervision, using only a single cascade, but the report has not yet been confirmed by the IAEA. Iran has also stated that it will stop the efforts to produce the 19.75 percent LEU, if the international community is willing to sell the fuel for the TRR.

Iran has also announced that it will set up 10 more uranium enrichment centers, in addition to its main enrichment facility at Natanz, which currently houses close to 8,000 centrifuges, and a small under-construction facility in Fordow near Qom that is supposed to eventually house 3,000 centrifuges, but will not come online for at least another 18 months.

But, amid the hysteria, few people are asking the relevant questions. Can Iran actually do what it has said it wants to do? If it can, at what speed? Does Iran have all the required technology and know-how to expand its nuclear program rapidly?

Prospects for a Nuclear Deal

Before answering the all-important questions, let us briefly review the state of affairs between Iran and the P5+1—the five permanent members of the United Nations Security Council plus Germany. On February 2 [2010], Mahmoud Ahmadinejad [Iran's president] declared on Iranian television that Iran had "no problem" with the third party enrichment deal's terms, and that the nation was willing to send its uranium abroad for further enrichment. He was talking about a deal whereby Iran is supposed to ship most of its stockpile of LEU abroad, and will receive in return the fuel for the TRR.

The deal had been agreed on in October in Geneva [Switzerland] between Iran's negotiation team and the P5+1 and the IAEA. But, when the deal was taken to Tehran for final approval, it generated strong backlash across the political spectrum, from the opposition to the conservatives. The opposition leader, Mir-Hossein Mousavi [Khameneh], declared that it was a terrible agreement, because if Iran does go along with it, it will lose most of its stockpile of the LEU, and if it does not, it will be punished by new sanctions.

Others thought that Iran's LEU was its bargaining chip that should not be lost easily. Still others thought that shipping the LEU abroad for further enrichment will become a permanent fixture of any possible future agreement between Iran and the P5+1, which is not acceptable to Iran.

Iran also wanted a simultaneous swap of its LEU with the fuel for the TRR. But the fact is that the TRR is old. The fuel for that type of reactor is not produced on a regular basis, nor is there much of it in any country's stockpile. In fact, only Argentina (that provided the fuel for the TRR in the past) and France can produce it. The P5+1 has been saying that it would take up to a year to fabricate the fuel, but it wants Iran to immediately ship out most of its LEU, and wait to receive the fuel. Iran seems to believe that it should only take a few months to prepare the fuel.

Still, Ahmadinejad and at least some of his allies want a deal. First, they are under tremendous pressure, both within Iran—due to the aftermath of the June 12 [2009] rigged presidential election—and by the international community over their regime's gross violations of human rights, imprisonment of thousands of people protesting the fraud in the election, murder of several dozen people, execution of at least 4 people, the assassination of two prominent members of the opposition, etc., not to mention Iran's nuclear program, even though it is a peaceful program, at least so far.

Thus, in Ahmadinejad's view reaching an agreement with the P5+1 will lessen the international pressure on his government, and might improve the relations with the United States.

The latter is also his goal, because he sees it as a way of gaining some credibility with the Iranian people living in Iran after losing all his credibility with a very large segment of the population, and at the same time giving them the message that the U.S. is not on their side, even though most Iranians reject any U.S. aid to the Green Movement in the first place. They do not want any intervention by the outside world, and particularly by the U.S., in their internal affairs.

But, the U.S. and its allies do not seem to be capable of taking yes for an answer. State Department spokesman P.J. Crowley said, "There is a forum to be able to resolve whether this [Ahmadinejad's offer] is a serious offer and that's through the IAEA. If Iran is serious, they can inform the IAEA that they are ready to accept the deal that's on the table. We are not prepared to change the deal. . . . We are not interested in renegotiating it. If Iran wants to accept it then they should inform the IAEA." German Chancellor Angela Merkel, who is so much in love with Israel that her cabinet and that of Benjamin Netanyahu, Israel's prime minister, recently held a joint session in Berlin, insisted that the time has come for tough sanctions against Iran.

Iran's Nuclear Program Is Very Limited

Let us now see whether Iran is actually capable of rapidly developing its nuclear program. The first question is whether Iran is technically equipped to produce 19.75 percent LEU. Based on the present knowledge about Iran's nuclear program, that is not a given. Certainly, Iran has acquired a considerable amount of experience and know-how on uranium enrichment, but it still has difficulty producing the 3.5 percent LEU smoothly. Iran's centrifuges malfunction on a regular basis.

In fact, the *Washington Post* quoted Mohammad Ghannadi [Maragheh], vice president of the Atomic Energy Organization of Iran, as saying that while Iran could try to produce the fuel itself, "There would be technical problems. Also, we'd never make it on time to help our patients."

Even if Iran could produce the 19.75 percent LEU on time, it would still need to fabricate it into fuel rods. But, Iran has no experience doing so. It may take quite some time to acquire the know-how. If Iran tries to use the knowledge that has been accumulated abroad, the safety of the reactor may be jeopardized.

Although in principle the Natanz facility can enrich the 3.5 percent LEU to 19.75 percent, the ... uranium enrichment facility in Esfahan is contaminated.

Third, although in principle the Natanz facility can enrich the 3.5 percent LEU to 19.75 percent, the yellowcake [refined uranium ore] that is converted to uranium hexafluoride (the main feedstock for enrichment) in the uranium enrichment facility in Esfahan is contaminated with molybdenum and other contaminants. After enrichment to 19.75 percent the same impurities and contaminants remain in the enriched fuel. Hence, not only severely contaminated fuel is produced (even at the 3.5 percent) that may be useless, but the centrifuge cascades are also contaminated.

This point is never discussed in the mainstream media, even though it is highly important. Moreover, France has the know-how to clean up the contaminated fuel, which means that even though Iran does not trust France, it has to be involved. Of course, with patience, skill, unlimited funds, and knowledge in materials science Iran can eventually produce the fuel, but that is years away.

Finally, can Iran set up 10 new uranium enrichment facilities? Not in the foreseeable future. The Natanz facility is supposed to house around 50,000 centrifuges, but that is still years away. Even a significant fraction of close to 8000 centrifuges that have been installed at Natanz is not working for various reasons. There is also no evidence that Iran has secretly manufactured a very large number of centrifuges that are not known to the IAEA.

The cries for military attacks on Iran are becoming loud, without any legitimate reason whatsoever.

Thus, what is Iran's point in declaring that it will set up 10 more enrichment facilities? First and foremost defiance in the face of tremendous pressure, both domestically and internationally. More importantly, as [American investigative journalist] Gareth Porter pointed out, by claiming that it will set up more uranium enrichment centers, Iran may be trying to deter any possible military attacks on Natanz and Fordow.

Therefore, once again, the cries for military attacks on Iran are becoming loud, without any legitimate reason whatsoever. The reason is clear: The U.S. and its allies do not want Iran to have any uranium enrichment program because the crux of the issue is that, any such facility will enable Iran to make nuclear weapons on short notice, if its national security and territorial integrity are threatened by foreign forces. But, that capability would make Iran unattackable, a prospect that is not acceptable to the U.S. and Israel. They want to have hegemony in the Middle East.

The net result of the war hysteria is to set back Iran's democratic movement, by giving Tehran's hardliners something to rally the nation, silent the opposition, and continue their rule.

Iran's Nuclear Weapons Program Is a Myth

Patrick Buchanan

*Patrick Buchanan is an American conservative political com-
mentator, author, syndicated columnist, politician, and broad-
caster who was a senior adviser to several American presidents.
He ran as a Republican candidate for president in the 1992 and
1996 primary elections.*

Did [White House press secretary] Robert Gibbs let the cat
out of the bag?

Last week [February 8, 2010] [Iranian president] Mahmoud Ahmadinejad told the world that Iran, unable to get
fuel rods from the West for its U.S.-built reactor, which makes
medical isotopes, had begun to enrich its own uranium to 20
percent.

From his perch in the West Wing, Gibbs scoffed:

"He (Ahmadinejad) says many things, and many of them
turn out to be untrue. We do not believe they have the capability to enrich to the degree to which they now say they are
enriching."

But wait a minute. If Iran does not "have the capability" to
enrich to 20 percent for fuel rods, how can Iran enrich to 90
percent for a bomb?

What was Gibbs implying?

Is he confirming reports that Iran's centrifuges are
breaking down or have been sabotaged? Is he saying that impurities, such as molybdenum, in the feedstock of Iran's centrifuges at Natanz are damaging the centrifuges and contami-
nating the uranium?

Patrick Buchanan, "Myth of the Iranian Nuke," *The American Conservative*, February 16,
2010. Copyright © 2010 *The American Conservative*. Reproduced by permission.

What explains Gibbs's confidence? Perhaps this.

According to a report last week by David Albright and Christina Walrond of the Institute for Science and International Security [ISIS], "Iran's problems in its centrifuge programme are greater than expected.... Iran is unlikely to deploy enough gas centrifuges to make enriched uranium for commercial nuclear power reactors (Iran's stated nuclear goal) for a long time, if ever, particularly if (UN [United Nations]) sanctions remain in force."

Thus, ISIS is saying Iran cannot make usable fuel for the nuclear power plant it is building, and Gibbs is saying Iran lacks the capability to make fuel rods for its research reactor.

Which suggests Iran's vaunted nuclear program is a busted flush.

Iran cannot make usable fuel for the nuclear power plant it is building, and ... Iran lacks the capability to make fuel rods for its research reactor.

ISIS insists, however, that Iran may still be able to build a bomb. Yet, to do that, Iran would have to divert nearly all of its low-enriched uranium at Natanz, now under UN watch, to a new cascade of centrifuges, enrich that to 90 percent, then explode a nuclear device.

Should Iran do that, however, it would have burned up all its bomb-grade uranium and lack enough low-enriched uranium for a second test. And Tehran would be facing a stunned and shaken Israel with hundreds of nukes and an America with thousands, without a single nuke of its own.

Is Iran Bluffing?

Is Iran running a bluff? And if Gibbs and Albright are right, how long can Iran keep up this pretense of rapid nuclear progress?

Which brings us to the declaration by Ahmadinejad on the 31st anniversary of the Islamic Revolution [Iranian Revolution in 1979], which produced this headline in the *New York Times*: "Iran Boasts of Capacity to Make Bomb Fuel."

Accurate as far as it went, this headline was so incomplete as to mislead. For here is what Ahmadinejad said in full:

"When we say that we don't build nuclear bombs, it means that we won't do so because we don't believe in having it.... The Iranian nation is brave enough that if one day we wanted to build nuclear bombs, we would announce it publicly without being afraid of you.

Iran's vaunted nuclear program is a busted flush.

"Right now in Natanz we have the capability to enrich to more than 20 percent and to more than 80 percent, but because we don't need to, we won't do so."

On Friday, Ahmadinejad sounded like [former U.S. president] Ronald Reagan: "We believe that not only the Middle East but the whole world should be free of nuclear weapons, because we see such weapons as inhumane."

Now, if as Albright suggests, Tehran cannot produce fuel for nuclear power plants, and if, as Gibbs suggests, Iran is not capable of enriching to 20 percent for fuel for its research reactor, is Ahmadinejad, in renouncing the bomb, making a virtue of necessity?

After all, if you can't build them, denounce them as inhumane.

Last December [2009], however, the *Times* of London reported it had a secret document, which "intelligence agencies" dated to early 2007, proving that Iran was working on the final component of a "neutron initiator," the trigger for an atom bomb.

If true, this would leave egg all over the faces of 16 U.S. intelligence agencies whose December 2007 consensus was that Iran stopped seeking a bomb in 2003.

The *Times* credited an "Asian intelligence service" for having ably assisted with its story.

U.S. intelligence, however, has not confirmed the authenticity of the document, and Iran calls it a transparent forgery. When former CIA [Central Intelligence Agency] man Phil Giraldi sounded out ex-colleagues still in the trade, they, too, called the *Times'* document a forgery.

Shades of Saddam seeking yellowcake from Niger [referring to forged documents showing Saddam Hussein tried to purchase uranium powder from Niger].

Are the folks who lied us into war on Iraq, to strip it of weapons it did not have, now trying to lie us into war on Iran, to strip it of weapons it does not have?

Maybe the Senate should find out before voting sanctions that will put us on the road to such a war, which would fill up all the empty beds at Walter Reed [an army medical center].

The International Atomic Energy Agency Is Suspicious of Iran's Nuclear Activities

Peter Crail

Peter Crail is a researcher for the Arms Control Association, an organization dedicated to promoting public understanding of and support for effective arms control policies.

Since its investigation of Iran's nuclear programs began during the latter half of 2002, the International Atomic Energy Agency (IAEA) has discovered a series of clandestine nuclear activities, some of which violated Iran's safeguards agreement with the agency.

Others did not, but have nevertheless raised suspicions regarding Iran's claim that its nuclear programs are exclusively for peaceful purposes. During the course of the investigation, Iran has failed both to disclose some of its nuclear activities to the agency and misled inspectors about others.

Iran, as a member state of the Nuclear Non-Proliferation Treaty (NPT) [Treaty on the Non-Proliferation of Nuclear Weapons], has an IAEA safeguards agreement allowing the agency to monitor Tehran's nuclear activities and facilities to ensure that they are not used for military purposes.

Based on interviews with knowledgeable officials, IAEA Deputy Director-General Olli Heinonen's Jan. 31 [2006] report to the agency's Board of Governors, and previous IAEA reports, this [viewpoint] describes some of the unresolved questions concerning Iran's nuclear activities as of Feb. 24 [2006].

Iran's Nuclear Programs

Tehran is developing a gas-centrifuge-based uranium-enrichment program and constructing a heavy-water moderated nuclear reactor. Both programs could potentially produce fissile material for nuclear weapons.

Gas centrifuges enrich uranium by spinning uranium hexafluoride gas at very high speeds in order to increase the concentration of the uranium-235 isotope. They can produce both low-enriched uranium (LEU), which can be used in nuclear power reactors, and highly enriched uranium (HEU), which can be used in certain types of nuclear reactors and as fissile material.

[Iran] is developing a gas-centrifuge-based uranium-enrichment program and constructing a heavy-water moderated nuclear reactor. Both programs could . . . produce . . . material for nuclear weapons.

Iran has a pilot centrifuge facility, which so far contains a cascade of 164 centrifuges, and is constructing a much larger commercial facility. Tehran has told the IAEA that the pilot facility will eventually contain approximately 1,000 centrifuges and the commercial facility will ultimately house more than 50,000 centrifuges.

Iran also has a uranium-conversion facility, which converts uranium oxide (lightly processed uranium ore) into several compounds, including uranium tetrafluoride and uranium hexafluoride. Heinonen reported that the country's current "conversion campaign," which began in November 2005, is expected to end this month [February 2010].

Tehran [Iran's capital] claims that it wants to produce LEU for its light-water moderated nuclear power plant currently under construction near the city of Bushehr, as well as additional power plants it intends to construct.

Iran says that its heavy-water reactor, which is being constructed in Arak, is intended for the production of medical isotopes. But the IAEA is concerned that Iran may use the reactor to produce plutonium, and the board has asked Iran to "reconsider" the project. Tehran has told the IAEA that the reactor is to begin operating in 2014.

The spent nuclear fuel from both light-water and heavy-water reactors contains plutonium—the other type of fissile material in use. But clandestinely obtaining weapons-grade plutonium from light-water reactors is considerably more difficult.

IAEA Demands

The IAEA Board of Governors has adopted a series of resolutions which call on Iran not only to comply with its safeguards agreement, but also undertake "transparency measures." The latter are not required by Tehran's existing safeguards agreement, but the agency argues that these measures are necessary to resolve certain issues concerning Iran's nuclear programs. For example, the IAEA has asked Iran to allow agency inspectors access to some non-nuclear facilities. Iran has provided some access to these facilities, but the agency has requested additional visits.

The board has also called on Iran to ratify an additional protocol to its safeguards agreement—a voluntary measure which augments the IAEA's investigative authority. Although Iran signed the protocol in 2003 and has allowed IAEA to operate under its provisions since then, the protocol still needs to be ratified by Iran's parliament before formally entering into force.

In addition, the agency has called on Iran to "reconsider" its heavy-water reactor project.

Uranium-Enrichment Program

Tehran has been conducting research on two types of centrifuges: the P-1 and the more advanced P-2. Iran acquired its centrifuge materials and equipment from a clandestine supply network run by former Pakistani nuclear official Abdul Qadeer Khan. Iran has not been fully forthcoming to the IAEA about either of these programs. The agency is concerned that Tehran may have conducted undisclosed work on both types of centrifuges and may also have an ongoing clandestine centrifuge program.

Iran's capability to produce enough centrifuges for its programs is unclear. A diplomatic source in Vienna close to the IAEA told *Arms Control Today* recently that Iran currently lacks the expertise to produce P-2 centrifuges. Tehran can build large numbers of P-1 centrifuges but not enough to meet the commercial centrifuge facility's planned capacity, the source said.

Procurement Efforts. The IAEA's investigation of these efforts has been hampered by Iran's lack of full cooperation. Tehran has both lagged in fulfilling IAEA requests for documentation and provided the agency with false information regarding its centrifuge procurement efforts.

The [International Atomic Energy Agency's] investigation of [Iran's nuclear research] . . . has been hampered by Iran's lack of full cooperation.

Iran has acknowledged receiving centrifuge components and related materials during the late 1980s and 1990s. Tehran has provided the agency with some information regarding these acquisitions as well as related offers from foreign suppliers.

According to a November 2005 report from IAEA Director-General Mohamed ElBaradei, Iran has recently provided the agency with substantial amounts of additional documentation regarding its P-1 procurement activities. This information appears to have resolved some of the discrepancies in Iran's previous accounts, but the IAEA has requested additional documentation. For example, Heinonen reported that "Iran has been unable to supply any documentation or other information about the meetings that led to the acquisition of 500 sets of P-1 centrifuge components in the mid-1990s."

Heinonen's report also says that Iranian officials' accounts of "events leading up to" the mid-1990s centrifuge deal offer "are still at variance" with accounts provided by "key members of the [secret procurement] network." The report provides no details about these discrepancies but does note Iran's claims that "there were no contacts with the network between 1987 and mid-1993."

Iran claims that it conducted no work on its P-2 centrifuge program between 1995 and 2002, but the IAEA is skeptical of this claim.

Ambassador Ali Asghar Soltanieh, Iran's permanent representative to the IAEA, told *Arms Control Today* Jan. 23 that Iran suspended work on the program during those years because Iran had not yet "achieved mastery" of the P-1 centrifuge.

However, this response does not appear to address the basis for the agency's concern. According to ElBaradei's September 2005 report, the agency suspects that Iran may have conducted undeclared centrifuge work because an Iranian contractor was able to make modifications for certain centrifuge components "within a short period" after first seeing the relevant drawings.

Additionally, ElBaradei reported in November that the agency is assessing documentation provided by Tehran indicating that an Iranian contractor who had worked on the program obtained related materials that the government had apparently not disclosed to the IAEA.

Heinonen's report states that the IAEA, after sharing with Tehran information "indicating the possible deliveries" of P-2 centrifuge components, asked Iran in November "to check again" whether it had received additional components after 1995. Both the Vienna source and a former Department of State official familiar with the issue confirmed that the IAEA's information originated with Buhary Syed Abu Tahir, a businessman who has been detained by Malaysia for his role in the Khan network.

Both sources also noted that Tahir only recently revealed this information, although he has been in custody since the spring of 2004. Tahir had no documentation for his claim, the former U.S. official added.

Enriched Uranium Particles. According to Heinonen's report, the IAEA is still investigating the origin of some LEU and HEU particles found in Iran by agency inspectors in 2003. Iran has admitted to enriching uranium to 1.2 percent uranium-235, but the presence of LEU particles enriched to higher levels has suggested that Iran may have conducted other centrifuge experiments that it concealed from the IAEA. Tehran claims that the particles in question came from imported centrifuge components.

IAEA inspectors took environmental samples from a location in the United Arab Emirates where centrifuge components from the Khan network were stored before being shipped to Iran. The samples showed no "traces of nuclear material," according to ElBaradei's November report.

A Western diplomat told *Arms Control Today* in November that the sample results indicate that the LEU particles did not come from these components—a finding that could contradict Iran's account. But according to interviews with a State Department official, Washington is almost certain that all the LEU particles found in Iran originated in Pakistan and believes that any further discoveries of undeclared Iranian-produced LEU would likely reveal previously concealed P-1 experiments, but no similar P-2 experiments.

ElBaradei reported in September 2005 that "most" HEU particles found in Iran by agency inspectors came from imported centrifuge components. Both the source in Vienna and a State Department source says that, for all practical purposes, the HEU issue has been resolved.

Uranium Mining

The IAEA is investigating questions about the ownership and operation of Iran's Gchine uranium mine. U.S. and European officials have told *Arms Control Today* that Iran's military or an affiliated organization might have been working at the mine in an effort to obtain an independent uranium source.

The [International Atomic Energy Agency] is also investigating several activities and documents suggesting that Iran may be attempting to develop nuclear weapons.

Plutonium

ElBaradei first reported in November 2003 that Iran had conducted plutonium-separation experiments. Iran first said that it completed this work in 1993 but later admitted continuing experiments until 1998. The agency is still investigating the matter.

ElBaradei stated in September that the IAEA has not received requested information regarding Iran's efforts to obtain equipment for hot cells, which are facilities that can be used to produce medical isotopes as well as separate plutonium from spent reactor fuel. ElBaradei reported that Iran has attempted to procure hot cells with specifications more consistent with plutonium separation than medical isotope production.

Iran says it is no longer attempting to build hot cells.

Possible Nuclear Weapons Research

The IAEA is also investigating several activities and documents suggesting that Iran may be attempting to develop nuclear weapons.

Uranium-Casting Document. According to Heinonen's report, Iran has shown agency inspectors a 15-page document detailing the procedures for reducing uranium hexafluoride to "metal in small quantities" and "casting . . . enriched, natural and depleted uranium metal into hemispheres." But the document did not "include dimensions or other specifications for machined pieces for such components," the report says, reiterating information ElBaradei first reported in November.

This revelation has generated additional concern about Iran's nuclear program because shaping uranium into hemispheres is used in developing explosive cores for nuclear weapons. The report acknowledges that the procedure is "related to the manufacture of nuclear weapon components."

Whether the document is evidence of a previously unknown Iranian capability is unclear. Iran has previously acknowledged that it was offered equipment for casting uranium but maintains that it has never received any such equipment. Tehran claims that the document had been "provided on the initiative of the procurement network," rather than at Iran's request.

During a January 2006 visit, Iran allowed agency inspectors to "examine the document again and to place it under IAEA seal," Heinonen's report says. Tehran, however, declined the IAEA's request to provide a copy of the document, according to the report.

Parchin Military Complex. According to ElBaradei's November report, Iran granted IAEA inspectors access to Iran's Parchin military complex Nov. 1, the inspectors' first visit since January 2005. The inspectors "did not observe any unusual activities in the buildings visited," but the IAEA is awaiting the results of environmental samples taken during the visit before assessing whether Iran conducted any nuclear activities there.

The United States and the IAEA have both expressed concern that Iran has been testing conventional high explosives at Parchin for use in an implosion-type nuclear weapon.

The report also says that the IAEA seeks additional visits to the site but does not say why. However, a State Department official told *Arms Control Today* in November that the agency may still have "suspicions" about Iranian activities at the site. The official also confirmed a November Agence France-Presse report that the inspectors saw a high-speed camera during their visit. Such cameras can be used to monitor experiments with high explosives, such as those used in an implosion-type nuclear weapon.

The United States and the IAEA have both expressed concern that Iran has been testing conventional high explosives . . . for use in an implosion-type nuclear weapon.

Other Possible Military Projects. The former State Department official confirmed press reports Feb. 22 that the United States acquired a laptop computer, believed to be of Iranian origin, containing information documenting what appear to be several related projects that may constitute evidence of a nuclear weapons program. The United States has provided this intelligence to the IAEA, the Vienna source said.

According to Heinonen's report, the agency received information describing the "Green Salt Project." "Green salt" is another name for uranium tetrafluoride, the precursor for uranium hexafluoride. The former State Department official also confirmed that the computer contained designs for a "small-scale" facility to produce green salt. The most recent documents related to the project are dated 2003, but it is not known whether the project ended at that time, the official added.

The intelligence also indicates that Tehran has conducted "tests related to high explosives and the design of a missile re-entry vehicle," Heinonen said. A State Department official told *Arms Control Today* in August 2005 that the United States has what it believes to be documentary evidence suggesting that Iran is attempting to develop a nuclear-weapon payload for its medium-range Shahab-3 ballistic missile.

The United States acquired a laptop computer . . . containing information . . . that may constitute evidence of a nuclear weapons program.

But whether and to what extent such a re-entry vehicle design would improve Iran's ability to deliver a nuclear weapon is unclear. The former State Department official said that a re-entry vehicle built according to the design that Libya obtained from the Khan network would be too small to hold a nuclear weapon. That acquisition has sparked concern that Tehran also may have obtained similar designs, but no evidence has emerged that Iran has actually done so.

Nevertheless, the official cautioned that "[n]ot enough is known about the Iranian bomb-making capabilities" to determine whether Iran is capable of building a warhead suitable for the re-entry vehicle described in the laptop documents.

Tehran responded to a December IAEA request for a meeting by dismissing the agency's recently acquired intelligence as "related to baseless allegations." But Iranian officials later agreed to meet with Heinonen Jan. 27.

During that meeting, IAEA inspectors provided Iranian officials both with a diagram "related to bench-scale conversion" as well as communications related to the Green Salt Project. The Iranians promised to "provide further clarifications [about the project] later" but "declined to address the other topics during that meeting," Heinonen's report says.

Apparently calling into question Iran's claims that its nuclear program has no military dimension, the report says that the uranium project, high-explosives tests, and re-entry vehicle design all have a possible "military nuclear dimension and appear to have administrative connections." This claim is based partly on the fact that the relevant documentation was all found on the laptop.

Lavizan-Shian Physics Research Center. According to Heinonen's report, Iran has increased its cooperation with the IAEA's investigation of a physics research center that operated between 1989 and 1998 at a site called Lavizan-Shian that had been connected to the Iranian Ministry of Defense.

Iran razed the site in late 2003 and early 2004, a move that raised suspicions that Tehran might be trying to cover up evidence of undeclared nuclear activities. However, ElBaradei reported in September that Iran provided information consistent with the government's explanation for this action.

ElBaradei reported in November that the IAEA wished to take samples from a trailer that had been located at the site and contained dual-use nuclear equipment. The agency also sought to interview Iranian officials who had been involved in the center's efforts to obtain equipment related to uranium enrichment, he said.

According to Heinonen, Iran provided IAEA inspectors with some requested information Jan. 26 regarding Tehran's efforts to acquire equipment with potential uranium-enrichment applications. The inspectors, however, were not allowed to interview a key official involved in the center's procurement efforts.

Iran did provide the IAEA with information regarding other dual-use acquisition efforts and allowed the inspectors to take environmental samples of some dual-use equipment, Heinonen said. The report says nothing about the trailer discussed in ElBaradei's report.

According to the former State Department official, the United States has "good reason" to believe that Iran has moved the research center elsewhere but added that Washington has no "evidence" that Tehran actually did so.

Polonium-210 Experiments. The IAEA has also not been able to resolve residual uncertainties regarding Iran's experiments involving the separation of polonium-210, which is a radio-isotope that can help trigger a nuclear chain reaction in certain types of nuclear weapons. ElBaradei reported in November 2004 that the IAEA is "somewhat uncertain regarding the plausibility" of Iran's claim that the experiments were not for nuclear weapons because the civilian applications of polonium-210 are "very limited."

Iran May Be Keeping Open the Option to Produce Nuclear Weapons

Paul K. Kerr

Paul K. Kerr is an analyst in nuclear proliferation for the Congressional Budget Office, a government research agency that provides economic data to Congress.

Although Iran claims that its nuclear program is exclusively for peaceful purposes, it has generated considerable concern that Tehran [Iran's capital] is pursuing a nuclear weapons program. Indeed, the UN [United Nations] Security Council has responded to Iran's refusal to suspend work on its uranium enrichment and heavy-water nuclear reactor programs by adopting several resolutions which imposed sanctions on Tehran.

Despite this pressure, Iran continues to enrich uranium, install additional centrifuges, and conduct research on new types of centrifuges. Tehran has also continued work on its heavy-water reactor and associated facilities.

Whether Iran is pursuing a nuclear weapons program is, however, unclear. A National Intelligence Estimate [NIE, a U.S. intelligence report] made public in December 2007 assessed that Tehran "halted its nuclear weapons program," defined as "Iran's nuclear weapon design and weaponization work and covert uranium conversion-related and uranium enrichment-related work," in 2003. The estimate, however, also assessed that Tehran is "keeping open the option to develop nuclear weapons" and that any decision to end a nuclear weapons program is "inherently reversible." Intelligence community officials have reaffirmed this judgment on several occasions.

Paul K. Kerr, *Iran's Nuclear Program: Status*, Washington, DC: Congressional Research Service # 7-5700, 2009. Reproduced by permission.

Iranian efforts to produce fissile material for nuclear weapons by using its known nuclear facilities would almost certainly be detected by the IAEA.

Despite . . . pressure [from the United Nations], Iran continues to enrich uranium, install additional centrifuges, and conduct research on new types of centrifuges.

Although Iran has cooperated with the International Atomic Energy Agency (IAEA) to an extent, the agency says that Tehran's action's have not been sufficient to alleviate all of the IAEA's concerns about Iran's enrichment and heavy-water reactor programs. The IAEA continues to investigate the program, particularly evidence that Tehran may have conducted procurement activities and research directly applicable to nuclear weapons development. . . .

Does Iran Have a Nuclear Weapons Program?

In addition to the possible nuclear weapons–related activities . . . Iran has continued to develop ballistic missiles, which could potentially be used to deliver nuclear weapons. It is worth noting, however, that Director of National Intelligence Dennis Blair indicated during a March 10, 2009, Senate Armed Services Committee hearing that Iran's missile developments do not necessarily indicate that the government is also pursuing nuclear weapons, explaining that "I don't think those missile developments . . . prejudice the nuclear weapons decision one way or another. I believe those are separate decisions." Iran is developing missiles and space launch vehicles "for multiple purposes," he added.

In any case, Tehran's nuclear program has also raised concerns for various other reasons. First, Iran has been secretive about the program. For example, Tehran hindered the IAEA investigation by failing to disclose numerous nuclear activities, destroying evidence, and making false statements to the agency. Moreover, although Iran's cooperation with the agency has improved, the IAEA has repeatedly criticized Tehran for failing to provide the agency with timely access to documents and personnel.

In addition to the possible nuclear weapons–related activities ... Iran has continued to develop ballistic missiles, which could potentially be used to deliver nuclear weapons.

Second, many observers have questioned Iran's need for nuclear power, given the country's extensive oil and gas reserves. The fact that Tehran resumed its nuclear program during the Iran-Iraq War has also cast doubt on the energy rationale. Furthermore, many countries with nuclear power reactors purchase nuclear fuel from foreign suppliers—a fact that calls into question Iran's need for an indigenous enrichment capability, especially since Russia has agreed to provide fuel for the Bushehr reactor. Moreover, although Tehran plans to develop a large nuclear power program, the country lacks sufficient uranium deposits—a fact acknowledged by Iranian officials.

However, Iran maintains that its enrichment program has always been exclusively for peaceful purposes. Tehran argues that it cannot depend on foreign suppliers for reactor fuel because such suppliers have been unreliable in the past. Iran also says that it has been forced to conceal its nuclear procurement efforts in order to counter Western efforts to deny it nuclear technology—a claim that appears to be supported by a 1997 CIA [Central Intelligence Agency] report. [Former Iranian vice president Gholam Reza] Aghazadeh has also argued that, although Iran does not need to produce fuel for the Bushehr reactor, the Natanz facility needs to be completed if it is to be able to provide fuel for the planned Darkhovin reactor.

Although few experts argue that there is no evidence that Iran has pursued a nuclear weapons program, some have documented Tehran's projected difficulty in exporting oil and natural gas without additional foreign investment in its energy infrastructure. And at least one expert has described Iran's inability to obtain nuclear fuel from an international enrichment consortium called Eurodif. During the 1970s, Iran had reached an agreement with Eurodif that entitled Iran to enriched uranium from the consortium in exchange for a loan.

Tehran's nuclear program has also raised concerns. . . . [because] Iran has been secretive about the program.

Iran's stated rationale for its Arak reactor has also been met with some skepticism. Tehran says it needs the reactor to produce medical isotopes and to replace the Tehran research reactor. However, that reactor is capable of producing such isotopes and has unused capacity. Furthermore, as noted, Iran has expressed the desire to obtain more fuel for the reactor. In addition, non-proliferation experts have argued that the new reactor would be unnecessary for producing such isotopes.

The 2007 National Intelligence Estimate

According to the 2007 NIE, Iranian military entities were working under government direction to develop nuclear weapons until fall 2003, after which Iran halted its nuclear weapons program "primarily in response to international pressure." The NIE defines "nuclear weapons program" as "Iran's nuclear weapon design and weaponization work and covert uranium conversion–related and uranium enrichment–related work." It adds that the intelligence community also assesses "with moderate-to-high confidence that Tehran at a minimum is keeping open the option to develop nuclear weapons." The NIE also states that, because of "intelligence gaps," the Department of Energy and the National Intelligence Council "assess with only moderate confidence that the halt to those activities represents a halt to Iran's entire nuclear weapons program."

The NIE also states that "Tehran's decision to halt its nuclear weapons program suggests it is less determined to develop nuclear weapons than we have been judging since 2005." The change in assessments, a senior intelligence official said December 3, 2007, was the result of "new information which caused us to challenge our assessments in their own right, and illuminated previous information for us to be able to see it perhaps differently than we saw before, or to make sense of other data points that didn't seem to self-connect previously."

According to press accounts, this information included various written and oral communications among Iranian officials which indicated that the program had been halted. The United States may also have obtained information from Iranian officials who defected as part of a CIA program to induce them to do so, as well as from penetration of Iran's computer networks. Additionally, the NIE also incorporated open-source information, such as photographs of the Natanz facility that became available after Iran allowed a tour by members of the press.

According to the 2007 NIE, the intelligence community assesses "with moderate-to-high confidence that Iran does not have a nuclear weapon." The community assesses "with low confidence that Iran probably has imported at least some weapons-usable fissile material," but still judges "with moderate-to-high confidence" that Tehran still lacks sufficient fissile material for a nuclear weapon.

On several occasions, the U.S. intelligence community has reaffirmed the 2007 NIE's assessment that Iran halted its nuclear weapons program but is keeping its options open. For example, Leon Panetta, director of the Central Intelligence Agency, did so in May 2009. Moreover, press accounts indicated that, as of September 2009, the community did not believe that Tehran has restarted its weapons program. The late-

September revelation of the Qom facility has increased suspicions that Iran may have restarted its nuclear weapons program. As noted, U.S. officials have indicated that the facility is likely intended for a nuclear weapons program. Nevertheless, administration talking points made public September 25, 2009, stated that the community still assesses that "Iran halted its nuclear weapons program in 2003."

Other factors also suggest that Iran may not have an active nuclear weapons program. First, the IAEA has resolved several of the outstanding issues described in the August 2007 Iran-IAEA work plan and has apparently not found additional evidence of a nuclear weapons program. Indeed, the agency has not discovered significant undeclared Iranian nuclear activities for several years (although, as noted above, the IAEA's ability to monitor Iran's nuclear facilities has decreased). Second, Tehran, beginning in 2003, has been willing to disclose previously undeclared nuclear activities to the IAEA (though, as previously discussed, Iran has not been fully cooperating with the agency). Third, Iran made significant changes to the administration of its nuclear program in fall 2003—changes that produced greater openness with the IAEA and may have indicated a decision to stop a nuclear weapons program.

On several occasions, the U.S. intelligence community has reaffirmed the 2007 . . . assessment that Iran halted its nuclear weapons program but is keeping its options open.

Fourth, as noted above, Iranian officials have stated numerous times that Tehran is not seeking nuclear weapons, partly for religious reasons—indeed, Khamenei has issued a fatwa against nuclear weapons, according to Iranian officials. A change in this stance could damage Iranian religious leaders' credibility. Moreover, Mark Fitzpatrick of the International Institute for Strategic Studies argued in May 2008 that "given the pervasive religiosity of the regime, it is unlikely that Iran's supreme leader would be secretly endorsing military activity in explicit contradiction of his own religious edict."

Fifth, Iranian officials have argued that nuclear weapons would not improve the country's national security because Iran would not be able to compete with the arsenals of larger countries, such as the United States. Moreover, the U.S.-led spring 2003 invasion of Iraq, which overthrew Iraqi leader Saddam Hussein and thereby eliminated a key rival of Iran, may also have induced Tehran to decide that it did not need nuclear weapons.

Living with Risk

Other findings of the NIE indicate that the international community may, for the foreseeable future, have to accept some risk that Iran will develop nuclear weapons. According to the 2007 NIE, "only an Iranian political decision to abandon a nuclear weapons objective would plausibly keep Iran from eventually producing nuclear weapons—and such a decision is inherently reversible." The estimate also asserted that "Iran has the scientific, technical and industrial capacity eventually to produce nuclear weapons if it decides to do so," adding that, "since fall 2003, Iran has been conducting research and development projects with commercial and conventional military applications—some of which would also be of limited use for nuclear weapons."

This is not to say that an Iranian nuclear weapons capability is inevitable; as noted above, Iran does not yet have such a capability. But Tehran would likely need to accept additional constraints on its nuclear program in order to provide the international community with confidence that it is not pursuing a nuclear weapon.

Other Constraints on Nuclear Weapons Ambitions

Although the production of fissile material is widely considered to be the most difficult step in nuclear weapons development, Iran would, even with the ability to produce HEU [highly enriched uranium], still face challenges in producing nuclear weapons, such as developing a workable physics package and effective delivery vehicles. A 1978 CIA report points out that there is a

> great difference between the development and testing of a simple nuclear device and the development of a nuclear weapons system, which would include both relatively sophisticated nuclear designs and an appropriate delivery system.

Although developing and producing HEU-based nuclear weapons covertly would probably be Tehran's preferred option, such a path would present additional challenges. A 2005 report from the International Institute for Strategic Studies concluded that "an Iranian planner would have little basis for confidence that significant nuclear facilities could be kept hidden." Tehran would need to hide a number of activities, including uranium conversion, the movement of uranium from mines, and the movement of centrifuge feedstock. Alternatively, Tehran could import uranium ore or centrifuge feedstock, but would also need to do so covertly. Furthermore, Iran could produce only fairly simple nuclear weapons, which are not deliverable by longer-range missiles, without conducting explosive nuclear tests. Such tests, many analysts argue, would likely be detected. It is also worth noting that moving from the production of a simple nuclear weapon to more sophisticated nuclear weapons could take several additional years.

Iran Has Recently Taken Another Step Toward Producing Nuclear Weapons

Howard LaFranchi

Howard LaFranchi is a staff writer for the Christian Science Monitor, *an international news organization.*

Iran took another step Monday [February 8, 2010] that will keep it high on the map of global nuclear trouble spots by announcing plans to begin processing its uranium stockpile to higher levels of enrichment.

Iran's intentions, announced in a letter to the International Atomic Energy Agency (IAEA), the United Nations' nuclear watchdog, sounded alarm bells among nuclear energy experts and international leaders working to curtail Iran's nuclear program because they represent another step in the direction of producing a nuclear bomb.

"This is worrying because it's another small step up the escalation ladder," says Daryl Kimball, executive director of the Arms Control Association in Washington. "What we have to keep in perspective is that Iran is still a number of years and a lot of technical expertise away from building a nuclear weapon," he adds. "But what's disconcerting is that they keep chipping away at those limitations."

Suspicions About Iran's Nuclear Program

Iran said in its letter to the IAEA that it plans to begin processing at least part of its stockpile of low-enriched uranium to 20 percent enrichment, a level considered "high-enriched" uranium and on the way to the 90 percent enrichment required for a nuclear weapon.

Iran says it needs the high-enriched uranium for a research reactor in Tehran to deliver isotopes for medical uses, and blamed the international community for leaving it no alternative by failing to reach an agreement for providing the nuclear fuel it needs.

Iran said . . . that it plans to begin processing . . . low-enriched uranium to 20 percent enrichment, a level . . . on the way to the 90 percent enrichment required for a nuclear weapon.

But several countries, including the United States, that thought they had a deal with Iran last October for providing the fuel say this latest step only raises additional suspicions about Iran's direction.

US Secretary of Defense Robert Gates, in Paris for meetings with French officials, said the international community has no alternative but the "pressure track" for influencing Iran's decision making—a reference to the Obama administration's efforts to obtain UN [United Nations] Security Council approval of a fourth round of economic sanctions against Iran.

French Foreign Minister Bernard Kouchner also said Monday that Iran's latest actions constitute "real blackmail," despite what he said are his doubts that Iran has the technical ability to achieve the level of uranium enrichment it speaks of in its IAEA letter.

Mr. Kouchner noted that all major powers except China are now on board the sanctions effort. Russia has recently indicated its support for additional sanctions targeting the economic interests behind Iran's nuclear program. And on Monday a prominent member of Russia's parliament and specialist in Russian foreign policy, Konstantin Kosachev, said the international community should "swiftly react" to Iran's latest plans.

Iran's latest announcement is the latest in a string of conflicting signals to the international community. Last week Iranian President Mahmoud Ahmadinejad said Iran was ready to accept a deal with world powers to export a large quantity of Iran's uranium stockpile for eventual reprocessing into fuel for the Tehran research reactor. Then on Sunday he gave the first hint of the enrichment plan announced today in the letter to the IAEA.

Iran's intention to reprocess an undisclosed portion of its low-enriched uranium to 20 percent enrichment causes new concerns but also calls for a dose of caution, nuclear experts say.

US Secretary of Defense Robert Gates, in Paris for meetings with French officials, said the international community has no alternative but the "pressure track" for influencing Iran's decision making.

In the "Concerns" Column

- If Iran does arrive at 20 percent enrichment on its own, the time and number of spinning centrifuges required to get to 90 percent enrichment—the level needed for a nuclear weapon—is less.

- Other sources exist for the fuel Iran supposedly needs to operate its research reactor, thus raising suspicions about Iran's stated reason for enriching on its own.

"The ostensible reason they are giving for this step is a problem because they simply don't need an industrial-scale operation to deliver the fuel" for the Tehran research reactor, Mr. Kimball says.

And in the "Cautions" Column

- Iran has said that it will allow the IAEA inspectors to stay. That means that the international community should be immediately aware of any further increases in the enrichment process.

- Iran still faces technical hurdles before it is capable of building and delivering a nuclear weapon, nuclear experts say.

- Iran is still "years" away from possessing a nuclear weapon, Dennis Blair, the director of national intelligence, told the Senate Select Committee on Intelligence last week.

"What that means is that there's still time for a diplomatic solution to this," Kimball says. "The problem is that right now the Iranians aren't acting too interested."

Intelligence Information Strongly Suggests That Iran's Nuclear Motives Are Not Peaceful

Dieter Bednarz, Erich Follath, and Holger Stark

Dieter Bednarz, Erich Follath, and Holger Stark are reporters for Spiegel, *a German news source.*

It was probably the last attempt to defuse the nuclear dispute with Tehran [Iran's capital] without having to turn to dramatic new sanctions or military action. The plan, devised at the White House in October [2009], had Russian and Chinese support and came with the seal of approval of the US president. It was clearly a Barack Obama operation.

Under the plan, Iran would send a large share of its low-enriched uranium abroad, all at once, for a period of one year, receiving internationally monitored quantities of nuclear fuel elements in return. It was a deal that provided benefits for all sides. The Iranians would have enough material for what they claim is their civilian nuclear program, as well as for scientific experiments, and the world could be assured that Tehran would not be left with enough fissile material for its secret domestic uranium enrichment program—and for what the West assumes is the building of a nuclear bomb.

Tehran's leaders initially agreed to the proposal "in principle." But for weeks they put off the international community with vague allusions to a "final response," and when that response finally materialized, it came in the form of a "counter-proposal." Under this proposal, Tehran insisted that the exchange could not take place all at once, but only in stages, and that the material would not be sent abroad. Instead, Tehran wanted the exchange to take place in Iran.

Once again, the Iranian leadership has rebuffed the West with phony promises of its willingness to compromise. The government in Tehran officially rejected the nuclear exchange plan last Tuesday [January 2010]. To make matters worse, after the West's discovery of a secret uranium enrichment plant near Qom, President Mahmoud Ahmadinejad defiantly announced that he would never give in, and in fact would build 10 more enrichment plants instead.

After an extensive internal investigation, [International Atomic Energy Agency] officials concluded that a computer obtained from Iran years ago contains highly volatile material.

Highly Volatile Material

But officials in Washington and European capitals are currently not as concerned about these cocky, unrealistic announcements as they are about intelligence reports based on sources within Iran and information from high-ranking defectors. The new information, say American experts, will likely prompt the US government to reassess the risks coming from the mullah [male religious leader]-controlled country in the coming days and raise the alarm level from yellow to red. Skeptics who in the past, sometimes justifiably so, treated alarmist reports as Israeli propaganda, are also extremely worried. They include the experts from the United Nations International Atomic Energy Agency (IAEA), whose goal is [to] prevent the spread of nuclear weapons.

After an extensive internal investigation, IAEA officials concluded that a computer obtained from Iran years ago contains highly volatile material. The laptop reached the Americans through Germany's foreign intelligence agency, the Bundesnachrichtendienst (BND), and was then passed on to the IAEA in Vienna.

Reports by Ali Reza Asgari, Iran's former deputy defense minister who managed to defect to the United States, where he was given a new identity, proved to be just as informative. Nuclear scientist Shahram Amiri, who "disappeared" during a pilgrimage to Mecca in June 2009, is also believed to have particularly valuable information. The Iranian authorities accused Saudi Arabia and the United States of kidnapping the expert, but it is more likely that he defected.

Iran's government has come under pressure as a result of the new charges. They center on the question of who exactly is responsible for the country's nuclear program—and what this says about its true nature. The government has consistently told the IAEA that the only agency involved in uranium enrichment is the National Energy Council, and that its work was exclusively dedicated to the peaceful use of the technology.

Officials . . . conclude that the government in Tehran is serious about developing a bomb, and that its plans are well advanced.

But if the claims are true that have been made in an intelligence dossier currently under review in diplomatic circles in Washington, Vienna, Tel Aviv and Berlin, portions of which *Spiegel* [a German news source] has obtained, this is a half-truth at best.

According to the classified document, there is a secret military branch of Iran's nuclear research program that answers to the Defense Ministry and has clandestine structures. The officials who have read the dossier conclude that the government in Tehran is serious about developing a bomb, and that its plans are well advanced. There are two names that appear again and again in the documents, particularly in connection with the secret weapons program: Kamran Daneshjoo and Mohsen Fakhrizadeh.

Secret Heart of Iran's Nuclear Weapons Program

Daneshjoo, 52, Iran's new minister of science, research and technology, is also responsible for the country's nuclear energy agency, and he is seen as a close ally of Ahmadinejad. Opposition leaders say he is a hardliner who was partly responsible for the apparently rigged presidential election in June [2009]. Daneshjoo's biography includes only marginal references to his possible nuclear expertise. In describing himself, the man with the steely gray beard writes that he studied engineering in the British city of Manchester, and then spent several years working at a Tehran "Center for Aviation Technology." Western experts believe that this center developed into a sub-organization of the Defense Ministry known as the FEDAT, an acronym for the "Department for Expanded High-Technology Applications"—the secret heart of Iran's nuclear weapons program. The head of that organization is Mohsen Fakhrizadeh, 48, an officer in the Revolutionary Guard and a professor at Tehran's Imam Hossein University.

Western intelligence agencies believe that although the nuclear energy agency and the FEDAT compete in some areas, they have agreed to a division of labor on the central issue of nuclear weapons research, with the nuclear agency primarily supervising uranium enrichment while the FEDAT is involved in the construction of a nuclear warhead to be used in Iran's Shahab missiles. Experts believe that Iran's scientists could produce a primitive, truck-sized version of the bomb this year [2010] but that it would have to be compressed to a size that would fit into a nuclear warhead to yield the strategic threat potential that has Israel and the West so alarmed—and that they could reach that stage by sometime between 2012 and 2014.

The Iranians are believed to have conducted non-nuclear tests of a detonating mechanism for a nuclear bomb more than six years ago. The challenge in the technology is to uniformly ignite the conventional explosives surrounding the uranium core—which is needed to produce the desired chain reaction. It is believed that the test series was conducted with a warhead encased in aluminum. In other words, everything but the core was "real." According to the reports, the Tehran engineers used thin fibers and a measuring circuit board in place of the fissile material. This enabled them to measure the shock waves and photograph flashes that simulate the detonation of a nuclear bomb with some degree of accuracy. The results were apparently so encouraging that the Iranian government has since classified the technology as "feasible."

Experts believe that Iran's scientists could produce a primitive, truck-sized version of the [nuclear] bomb [in 2010].

Spiegel obtained access to a FEDAT organizational chart and a list of the names of scientists working for the agency. The Vienna-based IAEA also has these documents, but the Iranian president claims that they are forged and are being used to discredit his country. After reporting two years ago that the Iranians had frozen their nuclear weapons research in 2003, the CIA [Central Intelligence Agency] and other intelligence agencies will probably paint a significantly more sobering scenario just as the UN [United Nations] Security Council is considering tougher sanctions against Iran.

Mulling Sanctions

When France assumes the council's rotating chairmanship in February, Washington could push for a showdown. While Moscow is not ruling out additional punitive measures, China, which has negotiated billions in energy deals with Iran, is more likely to block such measures.

China could, however, approve "smart" sanctions, such as travel restrictions for senior members of the Revolutionary Guard and nuclear scientists. Fakhrizadeh is already on a list of officials subject to such restrictions, and Daneshjoo could well be added in the future.

But the West would presumably be on its own when enforcing sanctions that would be truly harmful to Iran—and to its own, profitable trade relations with Tehran. The most effective trade weapon would be a fuel embargo. Because of a lack of refinery capacity Iran, which has the world's second-largest oil reserves, imports almost half of the gasoline it uses. Sanctions would trigger a sharp rise in the price of gasoline, inevitably leading to social unrest. Experts are divided over whether it would be directed against the unpopular regime or if the country's leaders could once again inflame the Iranian people against the "evil West."

This leaves the military option. Apart from the political consequences and the possibility of counterattacks, bombing Iran's nuclear facilities would be extremely difficult. The nuclear experts have literally buried themselves and their facilities underground, in locations that would be virtually impossible to reach with conventional weapons.

While even Israeli experts are skeptical over how much damage bombing the facilities could do to the nuclear program, the normally levelheaded US General David Petraeus sounded downright belligerent when asked whether the Iranian nuclear facilities could be attacked militarily. "Well, they certainly can be bombed," he said just two weeks ago in Washington.

Current
CONTROVERSIES

CHAPTER 2

Does Iran Want to Dominate Iraq?

Overview: Iran's Interests and Role in Iraq

Edmund Blair

Edmund Blair is a reporter for Reuters, an international news agency.

(Reuters)—Iran and Iraq's other neighboring countries meet in Kuwait on Tuesday to discuss Iraqi security and other issues.

Following are what Iranian, U.S. and Iraqi officials say about Iran's interests and role in Iraq, as well as analysts' views on Tehran's aims:

What Does Iran Say About Iraq?

- Iranian officials have called for the withdrawal of U.S. and other foreign troops, who they blame for destabilizing Iraq.

- Iran regularly voices support for the government of Prime Minister Nouri al-Maliki, who like most Iranians is a Shi'ite Muslim. Tehran says it is ready to help restore stability in Iraq, with which Iran fought a war in the 1980s.

What Do U.S. and Iraqi Officials Say About Iran?

- U.S. officials accuse Iran of funding, training and arming Iraqi militias. They say such operations are led by Iran's Qods force, a wing of the Islamic republic's ideological Revolutionary Guard. Iran denies the charges.

- Iraqi officials have urged Iran and its archfoe, the United States, not to fight a proxy war on Iraqi territory.

U.S. officials accuse Iran of funding, training and arming Iraqi militias.

What Are Analysts' Views About Iran's Aims?

- Analysts say Iran does not want Iraq to descend into chaos nor does it want U.S. forces to have an easy ride, which might give Washington ideas about military options against Iran.

- "They don't want (Iraq) to get out of control nor do they want it to be too comfortable for the (U.S.-led) coalition," said Iranian analyst Baqer Moin.

- Tehran is embroiled in a row over its nuclear program, which Washington says is a covert bid to make nuclear warheads, a charge Tehran denies. Although U.S. officials say they want a diplomatic solution, they have not ruled [out] military action.

- Analysts say Tehran wants a friendly Shi'ite-led government in power in Iraq but is also keen to ensure Shi'ite factions jostling for power rely on their neighbor as a broker, thus cementing Iran's influence.

- One example of how Iran has wielded its influence was by helping calm fighting that raged in recent weeks between the Mahdi Army militia loyal to Shi'ite cleric Moqtada Sadr and Maliki's government forces, analysts say.

- "They definitely do not want to see the Maliki government fall; that's why they negotiated the cease-fire . . .

but they don't want a complete area of stability and democracy in Iraq either because that would be a dangerous model," a Western diplomat said.

Analysts say Tehran wants a friendly Shi'ite-led government in power in Iraq.

What Are Iran's Official Ties with Baghdad and Washington?

- Tehran has not had diplomatic ties with Washington since shortly after the 1979 Islamic Revolution toppled Iran's U.S. backed Shah. But officials from both countries held three rounds of talks last year in Baghdad on Iraqi security. A fourth meeting has been delayed.

- Iran, unlike Arab states, has an embassy in Baghdad and Iranian President Mahmoud Ahmadinejad staged a high-profile official visit in March.

- Iraqi officials, including Maliki, have visited Iran where some leading Iraqi opposition figures lived in exile during the rule of former Iraqi leader Saddam Hussein.

Iran Has a Robust Plan to Exert Influence in Iraq

Joseph Felter and Brian Fishman

Joseph Felter is a national security affairs fellow at the Hoover Institution at Stanford University and former director of the Combating Terrorism Center at West Point. Brian Fishman is director of research at the Combating Terrorism Center at West Point and an assistant professor in the Department of Social Sciences at the U.S. Military Academy at West Point, New York.

Iran has a robust program to exert influence in Iraq in order to limit American power-projection capability in the Middle East, ensure the Iraqi government does not pose a threat to Iran, and build a reliable platform for projecting influence further abroad. Iran has two primary modes of influence. First, and most importantly, it projects political influence by leveraging close historical relationships with several Shi'a [one of two Muslim sects in Iraq] organizations in Iraq: the Islamic Supreme Council of Iraq (ISCI), the Badr organization, and the Dawa political party. Second, Iran uses the Iranian Revolutionary Guard Corps (IRGC) and Qods Force (QF) to provide aid in the form of paramilitary training, weapons, and equipment to various Iraqi militant groups, including Moqtada al-Sadr's Jaysh al-Mahdi (JAM) and the Special Group Criminals (SGCs). Iran also projects influence through economic initiatives and various religious programs. Iranian influence in Iraq is inevitable, and some of it is legal and constructive. Nonetheless, Iranian policy in Iraq is also duplicitous. Iran publicly calls for stability while subverting Iraq's government and illegally sponsoring anti-government militias.

Joseph Felter and Brian Fishman, *Iranian Strategy in Iraq: Politics and "Other Means,"* West Point, NY: Combating Terrorism Center at West Point, 2008. Reproduced by permission.

The History of Iranian Influence in Iraq

Although Iran publicly protested the U.S.-led invasion of Iraq in 2003, its agents and allies initially cooperated with U.S. forces. Iraqi refugee groups with deep ties to Iran participated in U.S.-sponsored pre-invasion conferences, and Iran urged its surrogates to assist U.S. forces and position themselves to seize power through the electoral process. Yet even as its political allies came to power in Baghdad [the capital of Iraq] with U.S. backing, Iran began supporting anti-government, anti-coalition militia movements typified by JAM and, later, the SGCs. The two-tracked strategy offered Iran unique levers to increase violence in Iraq and then to benefit when violence subsided. Another advantage has been that, intentionally or not, Iran's two-pronged approach obscured the importance of Iran's political influence in Iraq by focusing the international media and U.S. policy makers on Iran's lethal aid to militia groups.

Iran has achieved three major accomplishments in Iraq. First, the unstable security situation and political opposition means the U.S. is not in a position to use Iraq as a platform for targeting Iran. Second, Iran's political allies have secured high-ranking positions in the Iraqi government. Third, the Iraqi constitution calls for a highly federalized state. Iran values a decentralized Iraq because it will be less capable of projecting power, and because Iran is primarily concerned with Iraq's southern, oil-rich, Shi'a-dominated provinces. Iran believes that increased southern autonomy will leave those provinces more open to Iranian influence. Iran's successes in Iraq are not all a function of its own efforts. For example, a democratic Iraq will almost certainly be highly federalized because of the power of Iraqi Kurds to distance themselves from the Iraqi government, and because of increasingly heated sectarian divisions that can be mitigated by devolving power to regional governments.

Iran's effort to manipulate Iraqi surrogates predates the 2003 U.S. military operations. During the 1980s and 1990s, Iran helped organize and finance ISCI's predecessor, the Supreme Council for Islamic Revolution in Iraq (SCIRI), and its Badr Corps militia. It also worked closely with elements of the Islamic Dawa Party and helped train and fund its militant wing. Before 2003, the Badr Corps served as Iran's most important action arm inside Iraq, and was considered an official component of the IRGC-QF. Badr received training and weapons from the IRGC-QF and Lebanese Hizballah to attack both the Iraqi regime and the Mujahedin-e Khalq Organization (MKO), an Iranian terrorist group. Numerous senior individuals in the Badr Corps during the 1990s play critical logistical roles funneling weapons to militants in Iraq today, including Abu Mustafa al-Sheibani—the first major explosively formed penetrator (EFP) smuggler—and Abu Mahdi al-Muhandis, the terrorist and former Badr Corps commander who was elected to the Iraqi parliament before fleeing to Iran. In some cases, these people had direct ties to current Iraqi politicians, including Hadi al-Ameri, who was al-Muhandis's chief of staff.

Iran's support for Iraqi refugee groups in the 1980s and 1990s has important consequences today. The refugee groups often disagreed over how closely to associate with the Iranian regime. SCIRI was most closely linked to Iran's clerical regime, going so far as to recognize Ayatollah Khomeini's doctrine of guardianship of the jurist—*velayat-e faqih* [a type of government in which senior Islamic religious leaders, or jurists, exercise authority]—which implied Ayatollah [Ruhollah] Khomeini was their supreme leader. The Dawa Party, however, was bitterly split over *velayat-e faqih*. Meanwhile, many Shi'a that remained in Iraq grew resentful of the Iraqi refugees that pontificated about Saddam's regime without facing its brutality firsthand. Most supported Iran's religious government but rejected *velayat-e faqih*. The political and doctrinal disagreements were often reflected in debates about which religious figures to follow. SCIRI was led by Ayatollah Baqir al-Hakim, while many Dawa supporters and Iraqis still in Iraq supported Ayatollahs from the al-Sadr family. These divisions laid the groundwork for contemporary divisions between the establishment ISCI and Dawa parties in Baghdad and the anti-establishment Sadrist movement.

Iran's effort to manipulate Iraqi surrogates predates the 2003 U.S. military operations.

Despite its successes, Iran faces numerous hurdles projecting influence in Iraq. Many Iraqis—including Shi'a—despise ISCI, Iran's primary political ally, precisely because of its close relationship with Iran. In 2007, ISCI took its current name and abandoned the title Supreme Council for Islamic Revolution in Iraq, which had implied a closer relationship with Tehran [the capital of Iran]. ISCI also publicly stated that Grand Ayatollah Ali al-Sistani is its most important religious influence—thereby distancing the organization from Iranian supreme leader Ayatollah [Ali] Khamenei, whom it had previously considered supreme. Meanwhile, Iran's militia allies in Iraq tend to oppose Iranian political influence there. Muqtada al-Sadr and others are willing to accept Iranian training and weapons to pursue their political, religious, and criminal aims, but they remain hostile to Iranian political influence and thus are unreliable allies.

Key Findings

- Iran's primary strategy to influence events in Iraq since the U.S. invasion has been to support allies in the Iraqi political establishment. To do so, Iran has supported Iraq's electoral process and supported its Iraqi allies' political ambitions. An elected Iraqi government is the

U.S.'s best hope for a stable Iraq but also Iran's primary mode of projecting power in Iraq.

- The primacy of Iran's political strategy is particularly important now because of the political sensitivity of the U.S.-Iraqi negotiations on a Status of Forces Agreement (SOFA) and a Strategic Framework Agreement (SFA), which will govern the role of U.S. forces in Iraq after December 31, 2008. Iran likely prioritizes using supportive Iraqi politicians to influence the SOFA/SFA negotiations as a means to constrain U.S. freedom of action in Iraq over the long term, rather than increase violence now.

- Popular opposition suggests that Iraqi politicians will be more amenable to publicly support a SOFA/SFA after the Iraqi provincial elections, which were originally planned for October 2008, but will not occur until 2009.

- Iranian programs to support Iraqi militias are very robust. The IRGC-Qods Force, augmented by Lebanese Hizballah trainers, sponsor basic and advanced paramilitary training at camps in Iran and Lebanon. Iranian supplied weapons are being employed against Coalition and Iraqi forces, including the most lethal of improvised explosive devices (IEDs), known as explosively formed penetrators. Iran has supplied shaped IEDs that resemble EFPs to Iraqi opposition groups since at least 2001.

- The Iraqi government has cracked down on Iranian-affiliated militias in the last six months. The Iraqi government's effort does constrain Iran's ability to employ violence inside Iraq, but it will not prevent Iran from exerting influence through supportive Iraqi politicians.

- Iranian influence in Iraq can be beneficial when it is a force for stability and economic growth. Iranian pilgrims to Iraq's shrine cities bring in needed revenue; cross-border trade is natural and productive; even the presence of Iraqi politicians with strong links to Iran does not necessarily undercut Iraqi sovereignty or security. These politicians will serve an important moderating function when the inevitable disputes between Iran and Iraq arise.

- Iran will likely try to maintain a nongovernmental militant action arm inside Iraq for the foreseeable future, regardless of the political orientation of the Iraqi government or the presence of U.S. troops. These militant elements will serve both as a hedge against a potentially hostile Iraqi government and a lever to pressure any U.S. troops that remain inside Iraq.

- Muqtada al-Sadr is personally erratic and a determined opponent of the U.S. presence in Iraq, but his history of ardent Iraqi nationalism and support for a strong Iraqi central government means he is a potentially important bulwark against Iranian political influence in Iraq.

- Iran aims to evict all U.S. troops from Iraq. In lieu of achieving that goal, Iran will target U.S. troops and resources in order to demonstrate it has the capability to undermine the U.S. project in Iraq. At least one purpose of Iran's strategy is to demonstrate a credible deterrent against a U.S. strike on Iran's nuclear facilities. If the U.S. maintains a persistent force of any kind in Iraq, it should be structured to minimize Iran's ability to credibly threaten that force.

- Confrontations with the U.S., in Iraq and elsewhere, bolsters the political stature of Iranian leaders with their own constituencies.

- Some ISCI/Badr politicians will retain a close relationship with the Iranian regime for the foreseeable future. However, ISCI/Badr members, like all Iraqi politicians, will become increasingly independent of Iran as they are forced to cultivate a politically viable constituency within an Iraqi population suspicious of Iran. Many political leaders, including Prime Minister [Nouri] al-Maliki, a Dawa Party member, have shown promising signs of frustration with Iranian meddling in Iraq. Even superficial demonstrations of independence from Iran are positive developments that reflect the maturing of the Iraqi political process.

Iran aims to evict all U.S. troops from Iraq.

Key Recommendations

- *The United States should counter Iran's overarching Iraq strategy, not just its support for militias.* Whether designed as such or not, Iran's support for JAM and SGC has obscured its support for ISCI/Badr, as well as its political efforts to weaken the Iraqi central government. Victories over JAM and the SGC militias are important, but they will be pyrrhic if not coupled with a focused strategy to constrain Iranian influence in the Iraqi political system. This strategy must be built on a policy that clearly explains which forms of Iranian influence are acceptable and which are not acceptable. If the U.S. overlooks Iranian efforts to shape Iraqi politics and society, it may suffer a severe strategic setback even if violence in Iraq subsides.

- *The United States' strategy should use all forms of national power, including diplomacy, to counter negative Iranian influence in Iraq.* Iran has a relatively cohesive strategy in Iraq that coordinates military, economic, and diplomatic efforts. The U.S. strategy should be similarly nuanced and coordinated. Diplomatic efforts, including both direct negotiations with Iran and a stronger effort to coordinate Arab responses to Iran's meddling in Iraq should be a part of that strategy. A key diplomatic goal should be to increase transparency of economic development money spent in Iraq to ensure that Iranian-sponsored projects can be identified and are difficult to use as cover for more nefarious activities.

- *Encourage Prime Minister al-Maliki's increasingly nationalist views.* Prime Minister al-Maliki comes from a staunchly pro-Iranian wing of the Dawa Party; his recent crackdown on JAM and the SGCs is an effort to improve his party's electoral prospects in the provincial elections and to weaken al-Sadr politically. Although the crackdown is self-serving, it demonstrates the increasing importance al-Maliki places on a domestic Iraqi constituency.

- *Increase accountability in the Iraqi government.* Neither the United States nor Iraqi nationalists have effectively responded to Iranian infiltration of the Iraqi government through ISCI/Badr or the Dawa Party. One way to increase accountability is to force all Iraqi politicians to be directly accountable to specific constituents, whether by using single-member districts or allowing Iraqi voters to vote for individuals rather than political parties. Legislation to maximize transparency of government and political parties would enable and compel ISCI/Badr politicians to be more independent of their Iranian suitor.

- *Offer Muqtada al-Sadr incentives to participate in the Iraqi political process.* Muqtada al-Sadr is unpredictable and violent, but he symbolizes Iraqi nationalism for millions of Iraqis. The United States should not tolerate JAM violence, but should incentivize al-Sadr's participation in the Iraqi government; his presence serves as a counterweight to Iranian-backed groups that favor a federalized Iraqi state.

- *Target IRGC-QF operatives and logisticians in Iraq.* U.S. and Coalition forces should prioritize identifying and targeting Iranian agents who provide Iraqi militias such as JAM and special groups with training and weapons. Undermining the logistical support will have more significant, long-term effects than will strikes on rank-and-file militia members.

- *Support a Shi'a "Sons of Iraq" program to employ low-level JAM and SGC militiamen.* In limited cases, the Iraqi government and the U.S. should officially authorize former JAM and SGC members to support Iraqi Security Forces, in a program similar to the Sons of Iraq program. This will require developing some form of amnesty criteria commensurate with the program provided to former Sunni militants in exchange for cooperation. The Iraqi government should also embed professional cadres from the Iraqi Army for command, control, and monitoring.

- *Increase international public accountability for Iran's illegal activities in Iraq.* Sunshine is the best disinfectant. The government of Iraq should aggressively confront Tehran with evidence of Iran's illegal activities in Iraq and expose them broadly to the international community.

Iran Wants to Spread Its Influence in Iraq

Kimberly Kagan and Frederick W. Kagan

Kimberly Kagan is an author and the president of the Institute for the Study of War, a public policy research organization that studies military affairs. Frederick W. Kagan is a resident scholar and director of the Critical Threats project at the American Enterprise Institute for Public Policy Research, a conservative think tank.

Vice President Joe Biden recently [January 2010] told [TV talk show host] Larry King that Iraq "could be one of the great achievements of this administration." Mr. Biden's transparent attempt to take credit for [George W.] Bush administration policies aside, it's worth asking how exactly does the [Barack] Obama administration define success in Iraq?

Success in Iraq

Mr. Biden said, "You're going to see a stable government in Iraq that is actually moving toward a representative government," echoing President Obama's remarks at Camp Lejeune [a Marine Corps base in North Carolina] in February 2009. But he also said, "You're going to see 90,000 American troops come marching home by the end of the summer," echoing the only comment the president made about Iraq in last month's [January 2010] State of the Union address: "I promised that I would end this war, and that is what I am doing as president."

The problem is that progress in Iraq is not as inevitable as Mr. Biden suggests. Iraq faces a political and constitutional crisis weeks away from the most important election it will ever hold [referring to elections of March 7, 2010]. People working on behalf of Iran are actively seeking to spoil this election. They want to exclude Sunni leaders from the next government, align Iraq's Shiites [the second largest denomination of Islam] into a single political bloc, expel American forces, and create a government in Baghdad [the capital of Iraq] that is dependent on Tehran [the capital of Iran].

Success remains possible, but only if the Obama administration abandons the campaign rhetoric of "end this war" and commits itself to helping Iraqis build a just, accountable, representative government. It needs to establish long-term security ties that will bind our two states together, including the continuing deployment of American military forces in Iraq if the Iraqis so desire.

Many fundamental questions will be answered this year about how Iraq is to be governed that will shape its development for decades. Is the election free, fair and inclusive? Do all communities emerge from it with leaders who they feel represent them? Is there a peaceful transition of power? What is the relationship between the central government and provincial governments? What role will the military play in the evolving political system? Does Iran get to vet Iraqi political candidates? What relationship will the U.S. have with Iraq over the long term?

[Iran] seems to know what answers it wants regarding Iraq's future.

Iran's Influence in Iraq

Tehran seems to know what answers it wants regarding Iraq's future. Iranian officials, including President Mahmoud Ahmadinejad, Foreign Minister Manouchehr Mottaki and Chairman of the Assembly of Experts Ayatollah Akbar Hashemi Rafsanjani, worked doggedly in 2009 to rebuild the coalition of the three major Iraqi Shiite parties that had run in 2005 as a bloc. That effort failed when Prime Minister Nouri al-Maliki refused to join.

The Iranians then actively but unsuccessfully lobbied for Iraq's parliament to pass a closed-list election law in October 2009 in which the people could not choose particular candidates, seeking to increase their control of political parties and thus electoral outcomes.

On Jan. 7, 2010, when Foreign Minister Mottaki visited Iraq, the Accountability and Justice Commission (which was established in August 2003 to vet individuals who might serve in the government for links to the Baath Party [the party of former leader Saddam Hussein]) announced that it was banning more than 500 candidates from the upcoming parliamentary elections. They included some of the most prominent Sunni leaders who had been running on cross-sectarian lists.

Ahmed Chalabi, a leading member of the Iranian-backed Shiite list, helped drive the ban through the commission. So did Ali Faisal al-Lami. Mr. Lami was arrested in 2008 for orchestrating an attack by the Iranian proxy group Asaib Ahl al-Haq (AAH) that killed six Iraqis and four Americans in Sadr City. AAH splinters reactivated its military activities, after a yearlong cease-fire, by kidnapping an American contractor on Jan. 23. AAH is nevertheless running candidates such as Mr. Lami for parliamentary seats.

But politics is by no means Tehran's only sphere of influence in Iraq. The Iranian armed forces violated Iraqi sovereignty on at least two occasions in 2009—U.S. forces shot down an Iranian drone in Iraqi territory in March 2009, and Iranian troops ostentatiously seized an Iraqi oil well in December 2009 as the Iraqis completed a round of international oil bids.

The U.S. Response to Iranian Influence

Against this continuous Iranian campaign of engagement, intimidation and political machinations, the Obama administration has offered little more than moral support. In practical terms, this administration has done little to implement the nonmilitary aspects of the Strategic Framework Agreement (SFA) that would signal an American commitment to Iraq.

On the security side, the administration has wisely abided by the Iraqi insistence that we withdraw our forces from Iraq's cities, conduct all military operations only in partnership with Iraqi forces, subordinate all of our military operations to Iraqi legal processes, and generally respect Iraqi sovereignty.

But it has remained publicly inflexible about the withdrawal of U.S. combat forces and the ending of all U.S. combat missions by August of this year. Those specific requirements were imposed solely and unilaterally by the Obama administration and were never part of the international agreements between the U.S. and Iraq. The time line for drawing down U.S. forces and changing their mission in 2010 must be based upon the conditions on the ground, not arbitrary deadlines.

Against [the] . . . continuous Iranian campaign of engagement, intimidation and political machinations [in Iraq], the Obama administration has offered little more than moral support.

The U.S. has steadfastly refused to discuss a long-term military partnership with Iraq beyond 2011, despite the fact that the Iraqi military will not be able to defend Iraq on its own by then. It has refused fully to increase civilian efforts in order to accomplish tasks that had been performed by military forces now withdrawing. It has reduced funding for the Commander's Emergency Response Program, which allows the military to provide "urgent humanitarian relief and reconstruction" projects, as well as for other forms of humanitarian and security assistance.

Despite the vice president's many trips, the administration has consistently defined success as complete disengagement. Many Iraqi leaders interpreted the SFA as an indication that their country would develop a special relationship with the U.S. Instead, the Obama administration has given them every reason to believe that they will be—at best—just another country in the Middle East.

Success in Iraq has been very real, and there is every prospect that it can continue. Nevertheless, American military forces continue to play a vital role in Iraq's development. They are engaged in peacekeeping operations along the Kurd-Arab seam. They continue to support provincial reconstruction teams and, thereby, a large portion of the U.S. civilian efforts. They are the ultimate guarantors of the upcoming Iraqi elections. And they ensure Iraq's survival in the face of continuing Iranian military aggression. They also provide the U.S. with continuing leverage at a critical period in Iraq's political development, if we choose to use it.

Mr. Biden's comments and the administration's actions suggest that Iraq is on a glide path to success even as U.S. forces are on a glide path to withdrawal. The reality is different.

The situation in Iraq is dynamic and evolving, and the U.S. cannot take any outcome for granted. Active American engagement will continue to be vital to achieving a just, accountable, representative government in Iraq, especially as Iranian senior leaders actively attempt to undermine the democratic, secular and cross-sectarian political process that has emerged in Iraq since 2008.

Many Iraqis Object to Iran's Detrimental Actions in Iraq

Mohammed al-Qaisi

Mohammed al-Qaisi is an Iraqi journalist.

Iraqi politicians and rights activists are speaking out against Iran's detrimental influence in Iraq.

They accuse Iran of trying to sabotage Iraq's democracy and inciting sectarian violence through armed groups, Iran's al-Qods Force [part of Iran's military], and religious sermons.

Iranian Intervention in Iraq

The leader of Iraq's Sahwa movement, Sheikh Ahmed Abu Reesha, accused Iran of supporting terrorism.

"We have evidence of Iran's support of al Qaeda and terrorists, for facilitating the entry of drugs, and controlling Iraqi border areas and recruiting Iraqis to carry out operations that destabilize security," he said.

Abu Reesha added that Iran's humanitarian projects are designed for "hiding poison in honey, as they say. I am confident that Iraqis are not naive enough to allow Iran to deceive them with its projects, which pay a few dollars to make the world think that it is helping Iraq."

Director General of Water Resources Awd Thiab accused Iran of causing an environmental and health crisis by diverting the course of the al-Karoun River and by dumping waste.

"Iran is currently using the Shatt al-Arab [a river that borders Iran and Iraq] as a dump for refineries and sewage water, which has led to an increase in cancer cases in the south, especially in Basra," Thiab said.

Mohammed al-Qaisi, "Iraqis Condemn Iran's Influence in Iraq," Al-Shorfa.com, February 23, 2010. Reproduced by permission.

Osama al-Nujaifi, a member of the al-Iraqiya coalition, accused Iran of intervening in Iraq's internal affairs.

"We condemn such interventions and reject using natural, internal differences in Iraq for expansionist, imperialist projects, or in causing sectarian fitna [upheaval] or attempting to drag Iraqis to a fight in the name of sect or denomination," he said.

Al-Nujaifi added that Iran is attempting to increase its presence in Iraq as US forces withdraw.

"Iran's implementation of projects through fake companies and organisations affiliated with the Iranian intelligence agency and al-Qods Force is not accepted by Iraqi Shias themselves, as well as Sunnis and Christians," al-Nujaifi said.

Parliamentary leader of the Iraqi Front for National Dialogue Saleh al-Mutlaq said, "Iran wants to turn Iraq into a burnt-out region affiliated with it. It does not want any good for Iraq and does not want its democratic experiment to succeed."

"[Iran's] aim behind destabilizing security in Iraq is to keep world public opinion preoccupied with Iraq while it proceeds with the production of banned weapons and the possession of the atomic bomb," he added.

Iran is attempting to increase its presence in Iraq as US forces withdraw.

Iraqis Oppose Iranian Influences

Al-Mutlaq said Iraqis will not allow Iran to continue to intervene in their affairs.

"What are the charitable projects that Iran claims to be implementing in Iraq?" he said. "It is not giving a single dollar without having an illegitimate plan behind it in Iraq. The Iraqi boycott of Iran is the best proof of that. I know that these organisations are suffering from the boycott by Iraqis who reject the assistance given by them. This is reassuring, and I am optimistic that Iraqis themselves will uproot Iran from Iraq before the next government."

Iraqis said they reject Iran's attempts to intervene in Iraqi affairs.

Nasif Abdul Zahra, 54, a resident of Basra, said, "A few days ago, an organisation called the Association for the Assistance of Affected Iraqis said it would provide oil heaters for the winter season as well as medications. However, not one of us went there."

He added, "The truth is that all these Iranian organisations have started to unravel. They just seek to increase Iranian influence in Iraq, and in our turn, we told them that the best assistance you can render to us is to stop harming us and control your borders so that terrorists may not infiltrate through them."

Iraq Is Unlikely to Be Controlled by Iran

Max Singer

Max Singer is a senior fellow at the Hudson Institute and the Begin-Sadat Center for Strategic Studies. In addition, he is research director at the Institute for Zionist Strategies in Jerusalem.

From the beginning, the [George W.] Bush administration knew that the war in Iraq would be difficult, and the decision to launch the war was not easily taken. Administration officials were forced to choose between the risks of removing Saddam Hussein and the risks of leaving him in power.

Many experts warned that the Shia [one of Iraq's two Muslim sects] majority rule that would inevitably follow an overthrow of Saddam would mean the imposition in Iraq of Islamic fundamentalism, similar to that of Shiite Iran. It would also lead, they warned, to the suppression of Kurds and Sunnis [another Muslim sect], and a new ally for international Shia power. They argued that even if the Iraqi Shia leaders were not so inclined, they would still be dominated by Iran and the Shiite organizations that were funded, penetrated, and supported by Iran; and would be coerced through armed Iranian subversion.

So far, this has not happened. Iraqi Shiites are following the lead of Ayatollah [Ali al-]Sistani, who despite turmoil and pressure, stands firm in his support for free elections, nonclerical government, and decent treatment for all—Sunnis, Kurds [a non-Muslim ethnic group in northern Iraq] and secular leaders.

The current government, led by Prime Minister Nouri al-Maliki, is in the hands of a sectarian Shiite alliance that was

Max Singer, "A Hopeful Iraq: Two Dangers Averted," The Begin-Sadat Center for Strategic Studies, Perspectives Papers on Current Affairs, No. 43, May 21, 2008. Reproduced by permission.

formed during a period of sectarian violence provoked by the failed Sunni and Iranian efforts to create a civil war. The Maliki government has admirably shown it is not interested in following the paths of either Saddam Hussein [the former dictator of Iraq] or Ayatollah [Ruhollah] Khomeini [Iran's former supreme leader]. Rather, it appears committed to a pluralistic approach to government—the likes of which has not been seen in the Arab world for many years. Nor does the regime seem interested in a policy of persecuting or seeking revenge against the Sunni communities—although it has been slow to give Sunni leaders a greater share of power.

The Maliki government has admirably shown it is not interested in following the paths of either Saddam Hussein or Ayatollah Khomeini.

Basis for Fear

There are both real and exaggerated fears of Iranian domination of a Shia-led Iraqi government.

Iraqi leaders such as [Iraqi president Jalal] Talabani, [Iraqi politician Ahmed] Chalabi, [Shia political leader Muqtada] al-Sadr, Maliki, and [Iraqi politician Abdul Aziz al-]Hakim [now deceased] often meet with high-level Iranian leaders in Iran, and have generally refused to denounce Iran—leading many to claim that they are "agents" of Iran. It is well understood, as well, that no Iraqi leader can stand completely aloof from Iran. Iran's population is more than double that of Iraq, and it is led by an authoritarian government with a powerful, well-financed force of foreign agents, many of them operating inside Iraq. These agents have plenty of cash to spread around in a society where money buys power and influence, and they have the ability to eliminate those who they believe stand in their way. Indeed, many Iraqis have been murdered by Iranian agents.

Moreover, many Iraqi political figures have spent years in exile in Iran, and others have close family ties there, further making them subject to Iranian pressure. Iraqi Shiites also have more recently feared the possibility of a Sunni attempt to regain power in Iraq, with the help of the US and Sunni governments such as Saudi Arabia and Jordan. If Shia majority rule was in danger, Iran would be their only support.

All these factors provide a real basis for concern about the possibility of Iranian domination of Iraq.

Understanding Iranian Influence on Iraqi Leaders

On the other hand, one can dismiss many of these warning indicators. It is true that in effect many Iraqi players have kept a foot in both the Iraqi and Iranian camps—but that was to be expected, and does not mean that Iraq is falling into Iranian hands!

Consider the situation of any one of a number of Iraqi leaders who for years received financial or other help from Iran. Such a leader, now with some kind of political position in a free Iraq, was a potential source of Iranian influence. But he had his own power and income and the Iranians had to be afraid that if they demanded too much he would tell them "thank you very much for your past help, but things have changed." Such a person was interested both in preserving his independence and keeping his links to Iran, which were useful and in the future might become essential.

A few years ago nobody knew which way those with feet in both camps would go. If they acted as agents of Iran, then Iran would dominate Iraq. Now, five years after the liberation of Iraq from Saddam Hussein, after the creation of an Iraqi constitution and two elected Iraqi governments, and after the defeat of al Qaeda in Iraq, it is becoming increasingly clear that most of these leaders remain primarily loyal to Iraq. While many of them do maintain connections with Iran, they are not turning out to be reliable Iranian agents. The Iranians have had to recognize they can only maintain their connection by not asking too much.

These Iranian "agents of influence" in Iraq will prevent Iraq from acting against Iran, but they will not enable Iran to subvert the government of Iraq. A large number of Iraqi leaders will probably maintain significant relationships with the Iranian regime. A few will be almost completely compliant with the Iranians. Others will pay only perfunctory attention to Iranian attempts at influence. Most will be scattered along the spectrum of degree of Iranian influence.

Iranian Agents in Iraq

The Iranians have another source of power in Iraq. In addition to well-funded political agents, they support hundreds of armed agents, many in criminal gangs, especially in southern Iraq. The Iranian Revolutionary Guard [Corps] has operated such agents in many European countries where they have killed numerous Iranians deemed threats to Iranian interests. It is much easier for them to operate next door in Iraq, using the many Iraqis who have lived in Iran for years. These agents are used to fight against the US, but they are also potentially available to influence Iraqi politics.

However, similar to the decline in Iranian political influence, this source of Iranian power is also growing weaker. The gangs recently received a heavy blow in Basra and the south where the British had allowed them almost free rein, and they are not dominating the political scene in Baghdad.

The Iraqi government's recent action to bring law and order to Basra exposed the strange coalition dominating the city—criminal gangs, Iranian agents, and Muslim extremists. Due to the British Army's unwillingness to maintain law and order, this three-party coalition has been controlling the city and making life miserable for its residents. While impoverished Shiites of southern Iraq are glad to be rid of criminal gangs and fanatic Muslim enforcers, they also care about getting enough to eat and are not convinced that Maliki cares about their needs.

Iraqi Power

Thus far, the fears of Iranian domination are not materializing. In fact, it can reasonably be argued that the opposite is true: We are beginning to see signs of Iraqi Shiite independence and even blowback against the Iranians. Led by Ayatollah Sistani, Iraqi Shiism (which theologically is traditional Shiism) is beginning to be considered as an alternative source of religious authority in Iran. A Shiite Iraq is beginning to look more like a rival to Iran than like an addition to Iranian Shia power. Ayatollah Sistani was not willing to see Iranian President Mahmoud Ahmadinejad during his brief trip to Iraq in March 2008, and Iraqi demonstrations against Ahmadinejad kept him away from the Shiite holy city of Najaf.

While the fears of Iranian domination of Iraq are so far unrealized, the story is not yet over. In Iraq, as in most of the world, political leaders support those who they perceive will be the winner. Iran's failure to dominate Iraq results from the expectation that Iraq will continue to be independent and protected by the US. If that expectation changes, and the common view becomes that Iran will be the dominant voice in the region, many Iraqis will pay more attention to Iranian suggestions. This could result in an intensified struggle in Iraq and perhaps a drastic change in the current situation.

> *Fears of Iranian domination are not materializing. In fact ... we are beginning to see signs of Iraqi Shiite independence and even blowback against the Iranians.*

The other serious danger is deadlock in the Iraqi government, rendering it unable to carry out essential actions. The Iraqis—like the US when it first achieved independence—

avoided the need to compromise by agreeing to act by consensus. This assured all parties that their interests would not be trampled on. However, a system in which nothing happens unless everyone agrees is vulnerable to deadlock.

While this is still a danger, the confidence and respect that Maliki has gained by his initiative and success in Basra makes it more likely that Iraqi politicians will allow him enough freedom of action to limit harm from deadlock.

Iran Lost in the 2010 Iraqi Elections

Trenton Daniel and Leila Fadel

Trenton Daniel is a staff writer for the Miami Herald, *owned by* McClatchy Newspapers. *Leila Fadel is McClatchy's bureau chief in Baghdad, Iraq.*

The pro-Iranian party that's dominated Iraq's political life since the U.S-sponsored election in 2005 suffered a huge loss in last Saturday's [January 30, 2010] provincial elections, while Prime Minister Nouri al-Maliki's political party was a comfortable front-runner in a majority of Iraq's provinces, according to preliminary results Thursday.

A Loss for Iraq

The defeat of the Islamic Supreme Council of Iraq suggests that many voters, particularly in Iraq's Shiite Muslim south, abandoned a party that favored decentralization and is widely viewed as an arm of neighboring Iran in favor of a nationalist party that advocates a strong central state.

Maliki's party won a plurality in nine of the 14 provinces that held elections.

The Supreme Council's loss was most significant in the nation's capital, where Maliki's State of Law Coalition captured 38 percent of the votes to 5.4 percent for the Supreme Council of Iraq, the preliminary results showed. Maliki's party also did exceptionally well in Basra, the commercial center in southern Iraq, winning 37 percent, well ahead of the second-placed ruling Fadhila (Virtue) Party, which won 3.2 percent.

Maliki's Islamist Dawa Party had been the weakest of Iraq's Shiite parties. Now he's the most powerful Shiite political leader in the country, and a figure who's won both Sunni Muslim and Shiite support.

Many voters [in Iraq's January 2010 provincial elections] ... abandoned a party that favored decentralization and is widely viewed as an arm of neighboring Iran.

Maliki's party won the most votes in all of the nine highly contested southern provinces but one. He failed, however, to secure an absolute majority anywhere, not surprising in view of the dozens of parties that were competing. The Supreme Council of Iraq, by comparison, was knocked off its throne as the most powerful Shiite party in the country, taking second and third places in most of the southern provinces.

"They lost because they were about to create a ministate from the nine (predominantly Shiite) provinces in southern Iraq. Even the Shiites dislike this idea," said Sami al-Askari, a Shiite legislator who's close to Maliki. "They have close ties to the Iranians, and most Iraqis don't like the Iranians."

Maliki's popularity has risen over the past year after his military crackdown down on Shiite militias in southern Iraq and Baghdad. An Islamist, Maliki recast himself as a national leader and promised to build a strong central government. His critics charge that he's poised to become a dictator.

"If we correctly interpret the message sent by the voter, then many things will change," said Dhia al-Shakarchi, a prominent member of the Dawa Party. "Frankly, the people did not vote for Dawa, they voted for Maliki, and that is because he has distanced himself lately from the principle of politicizing religion. He has turned away from the Supreme Council."

Maliki was urgently summoned on Thursday to the holy city of Najaf by Iraq's top Shiite spiritual leader, Grand Ayatollah Ali al-Sistani. Officials close to Sistani and Maliki's Dawa Party said that Sistani wanted to discuss the possibility of Maliki forming an alliance with the Supreme Council.

An Islamist, [Prime Minister Nouri al-]Maliki recast himself as a national leader and promised to build a strong central government.

Maliki sought the backing of tribes across the country—Sunnis and Shiites alike—by appealing to them as an Iraqi nationalist and with government cash under the guise of paying them to maintain security. His bold military gamble last year in Basra and Baghdad [the capital of Iraq], which strengthened the authority of the central government, appears to have drawn further appeal as an alternative to the Supreme Council of Iraq, which sought to combine the predominantly Shiite provinces into a more autonomous Shiite state in the south resembling the semiautonomous Kurdish region in the north.

"It wasn't just about local issues; it was about federalism versus central government," Askari said. "Maliki showed himself as an Iraqi leader, not a Shiite Islamist. . . . The Iraqis are looking for a strong leader."

In the western province of Anbar, the Awakening Council—the group of Sunni tribal leaders who were backed by the U.S. military to weed out al Qaeda in Iraq—threw its weight behind Maliki.

"We're afraid of dividing the country. We wish the government would boycott Iran and close the borders," said Abdul Jabbar Abu Risha, a founding member of the Awakening Council in Anbar whose followers are running for provincial representation in the Sunni west. "We have trust in Nouri al-Maliki."

A Peaceful Election

The preliminary results were released Thursday evening at a news conference in the Green Zone, the heavily fortified 5.6-square-mile area in Baghdad. They covered 90 percent of the voting population in the four provinces, which excluded the predominantly Kurdish north. The other 10 percent come from Iraqi troops, hospital workers, prisoners and others who were required to vote early.

The provincial elections last Saturday saw a crowded race of more than 14,400 candidates vying for some 440 seats. Many of the office seekers pledged to help rebuild Iraq after the internal war that followed the U.S.-led invasion and ouster of dictator Saddam Hussein in 2003.

The provincial councils are responsible for controlling local security forces, naming governors and influencing the local appointments of ministry officials. Their power is limited; parliament in Baghdad can depose leaders, and money is allocated from the central budget.

In Nineveh province, the Sunni Arab nationalist party al-Hadbaa won with 48.8 percent of the vote, ousting Kurdish parties, which had been in control.

"We are not surprised," said Sheik Abdullah al-Yawar, a Hadbaa Party leader. "We are confident, we have patriotism and we thank God for everything."

The Kurds have 31 of 41 seats on the outgoing provincial council.

In Anbar province, the results were so close that it was too difficult to determine who'd emerge as the Sunni leader of the west.

The Awakening Council led by Ahmed Abu Risha made its debut as a political entity and took about 17 percent in the preliminary results, one of the top winners. Tensions are running high in the province, with Abu Risha and other Sunni Arab tribal leaders accusing the incumbent, the Iraqi Islamic Party, of fraud.

They showed McClatchy [a U.S. news organization] more than 80 polling-result forms that didn't match the final vote count that was sent to Baghdad. The electoral commission is investigating.

Despite fears that the results would spark violence, Abu Risha urged his followers to remain calm.

"We will not make your blood cheap," he said at his guest-house Thursday in the provincial capital. "All of you are relatives. Do not kill your cousins. I want self-restraint, and I don't want one bullet."

The top vote-getters in Anbar—Abu Risha and Saleh al-Mutlaq, the leader of the Gathering for the Iraqi National project—plan to announce an alliance Friday.

In Basra, where political parties battled for control of the oil hub in the south, the Islamic Fadhila (Virtue) Party lost control of the only province it had dominated. The party has 12 seats on the provincial council now but received only 3.2 percent in the preliminary count. Maliki's party swept with 37 percent of the vote.

Iraq's Future Is Unclear

Sarah Price and Nizar Latif

Sarah Price and Nizar Latif are journalists based in the Middle East.

The current U.S.-Iraq Status of Forces Agreement (SOFA) dictates that U.S. troops must vacate Iraq by December 31, 2011, although it is understood that there may be as many as 70,000 troops left behind as "advisers and trainers"; and a referendum is expected in Iraq in mid-2009 that may require U.S. troops to leave 18 months earlier. Nevertheless, however the U.S. occupation ends, it is expected that this is when the next battle for control of Iraq will begin.

Shia Influence in Iraq

Muqtada al-Sadr's Mahdi Army [a pro-Iran paramilitary force made up of Shias, a branch of Muslims in Iraq] was formed in Iraq in June 2003, but came to prominence the following year, after a major military conflict with U.S. troops in the Battle of Najaf.

The Sunni [another branch of Muslims in Iraq] paramilitary force has maintained its influence in Iraq, and has been a factor in ameliorating the level of violence through al-Sadr's cease-fire declarations.

Last November [2009], he demanded that all U.S. troops leave Iraq unconditionally, or he would lift the cease-fire and "support the resistance against the occupier." However, last summer al-Sadr announced plans to expand the army into a social, political, and religious organization, while still maintaining the militia.

He has left Iraq to study in Iran, raising questions about his continued authority, and whether Iranian President Mahmoud Ahmadinejad is seeking to bring his own influence to the new Iraq. Who has the power now, and who will have it later, is debatable.

Abu Raed, 44, is a former commander in the Mahdi Army, in the al-Ameen district in east Baghdad. He recently left the militia and is now a member of the Sadrist Independent Liberals political bloc.

He believes the U.S. made its first mistake in Iraq when it invaded and occupied a country it didn't understand. "Their worst failure was when they tried to divide Iraq into three states: northern, southern and middle, in order to weaken and control Iraq," he says, adding that [George W.] Bush wasn't expecting the level of resistance that came from the various militias that rose up in Iraq, following the invasion.

"We have not benefited from the occupation—we only got killing, displacement, and robbing Iraqi money and oil," he says. "I believe life will improve greatly with the exit of the American occupation."

He also believes the Mahdi Army is the solution for improving Iraqi lives: "The Iraqi people are currently waiting for relief, and we find the al-Sadrist line is the salvation and sanctuary to the Iraqi people because it is a line of Arabic people. Many of [al-Sadr's] followers have been thrown into prison, but we won in the last election in many Iraqi provinces, and we have the ability to return to the political arena in the next elections."

28-year-old Malik al-Mohammadawi is a former Mahdi Army fighter who now works in a milk factory in east Baghdad, and is married with children, but still holds the beliefs of a Sadrist follower.

"When the Americans leave, life will become normal, business will return, and Iraq will become more secure than ever before, because the cause of evil and chaos is the U.S. occupation, which wanted to make Iraq a client state. The Americans tried in various ways to eliminate the Mahdi Army, but they failed in their efforts, despite the support of police forces and the Iraqi army. To the U.S. forces, we were still strong."

But, he says, when al-Sadr called for a cease-fire and asked his militia to stop all military operations against U.S. troops, it opened the door wide for the U.S. forces to hunt down the Sadrists, but says they did what they could to ensure that not all of them would be caught, and he still believes in al-Sadr's influence over the Iraqi people.

"I have a great belief that al-Sadr can keep the unity of Iraq and its people, and he can stop the calls for dividing Iraq, and stop the spirit of sectarian division."

But Dr. Malik al-Noimee, a specialist in the study of the militias in Iraq, disagrees about al-Sadr's power in the communities. He believes that with al-Sadr's decision to expand the Mahdi Army from a militia into an organization that also has social, religious and political sects, he is trying to imitate Hassan Nasrallah, commander of Hezbollah in Lebanon.

The Waning Power of Militias

"The power of the Mahdi Army in the community is close to zero," he says. "There is no effect and a lot of militia members in the past are now wearing uniforms and they were forbidden to before. I am afraid that leaving the Mahdi Army without observing and without control measures by the government will not lead to canceling this phenomenon, and we must exploit this situation. The Iraqi government has to establish new values to replace the sense and ideas belonging to the militia in the Iraqi community, because now militias are closer to death than life."

He also doubts al-Sadr's influence at election polls. "The election results gave a clear size of the popularity of Muqtada al-Sadr in Iraq, although there is a part of those who elected [the Independent Liberals] who are not necessarily in favor of Muqtada al-Sadr; in their eyes, they made the situation worse and there were a lot of missed opportunities for the people of the southern region, in the field of construction and progress."

A U.S. study in 2007 estimated the Mahdi Army force was about 60,000 strong. But al-Noimee believes if al-Sadr called his militia to action today, only about a quarter of that number would show up.

"If Muqtada al-Sadr ordered them to fight, not more than 15,000 fighters would show on the scene." He also notes that the leaders of the Mahdi Army are driven much more by money than by religious ideology, and that an improvement in Iraq's economy could actually hurt the Mahdi Army's popularity and influence.

"The first factor is the strength of the central government, and the prestige of the government in a citizen militia, and then across the country in general; the second is the economic factor: If the government immediately improves the economy of the individual and the national economy, then Muqtada al-Sadr will never get people who listen to him from the communities that are considered the source of militias, such as the poor communities." He claims that many of the Mahdi Army leaders have links to Iran, and that it is having a source of money that really keeps them invested in the cause. "[There are] a very few who are driven by religious passion."

After the departure of U.S. troops, Iran would be a stronger influence on the Iraqi arena. . . . But, Iraq remains an independent, free country.

Iranian Influence

With al-Sadr now living in Iran, there are questions as to his continued influence—but also to Ahmadinejad's increasing persuasion—in Iraq, as Ahmadinejad tries to widen his power across the region.

Abu Raed thinks this is a temporary situation, and one that will be alleviated once the U.S. troops leave: "Iran has very clear power on the Iraqi arena by virtue of its relationship with some Islamic parties, which found Iran to be a safe haven, when they were being pursued by Saddam Hussein. Therefore, those parties have roots and links with Iran one way or another.

"I think that after the departure of U.S. troops, Iran would be a stronger influence on the Iraqi arena, by virtue of being a neighbor, an Islamic state, and as a Shiite sectarian. But, Iraq remains an independent, free country.

"There is a difference between Ahmadinejad, who is the leader of a political and military fields and al-Sadr, the religious and spiritual leader for most of the Shiites in the region. I do not think there will be conflict between them."

Al-Mohammedawi agrees: "I imagine that Iran has a major intervention in Iraq by virtue of their many parties on the Iraqi arena, as well as their relationship to those who are of Iranian origin in Iraq, and who are not ashamed, and they do not hide their links to Iran," he says. "But after the departure of the Americans, I believe that the Iranian influence will be less than ever before, because Iran now interferes because of their fearing that U.S. troops should stay close to its borders.

"If the U.S. troops are gone, Iran will pull its hands out of Iraq, and its relations will remain good, based on good-neighborliness."

But independent Iraqi parliament member Dr. Haider al-Sewedi is not so sure.

"The Iranian influence is very significant," he says. "There is a hidden conflict between al-Sadr and Ahmadinejad, because Ahmadinejad is trying to strengthen Iran's influence in the region, but al-Sadr doesn't accept any external interference in the Iraqi affairs, even if it is a Shiite state like Iran. Al-Sadr sought asylum in Iran in terms of security, only to save his life from the U.S. military. Now al-Sadr has little effect in the Iraqi arena."

With so many disparate opinions about who holds the power now in Iraq, only time will tell who will step forward as a leader after the pullout of U.S. troops in 2011—or whether anyone will have enough power to step forward at all.

CHAPTER 3

Will the Iranian Green Revolution Succeed?

Chapter Preface

The Green Movement, also known as the Green Revolution, refers to a protest movement that began in Iran following the country's presidential election held on June 12, 2009. Green was the symbol of one of the presidential candidates—Mir-Hossein Mousavi Khameneh, an Iranian politician who had earlier served as prime minister of the country (1981–1989). In the 2009 presidential campaign, Mousavi ran on a reform platform that promised to promote social justice and freedom of expression, to end government corruption, and to create a better economy. Mousavi and his supporters believed he would win, but official government election results reported that incumbent president Mahmoud Ahmadinejad, a conservative elected in 2005, had instead won overwhelmingly with about two-thirds of the vote. Mousavi and many others in Iran saw these results as election fraud, and soon thousands of Mousavi's supporters hit the streets around the country in a massive peaceful protest—wearing the color green and chanting slogans such as "Where is my vote?" and "Death to the dictator." The protestors have included students, women, and human rights and political activists, many of them under the age of 30—a bloc that currently makes up 70 percent of the Iranian population.

The Iranian government responded to the protests with a brutal, violent crackdown. Government police and militia beat and teargassed protestors and made hundreds of arrests. The government also banned further protests, blocked or slowed Internet access, and prohibited any media from attending or reporting on the demonstrations. This repression, however, only stoked the anger of the protesters and led to more widespread protests as days and weeks passed. Iran does not have a free press, and the government restricted the access of foreign and Iranian media to the protestors, so most of the information, films, and photos of the demonstrations came from the protestors themselves, who recorded images on their cell phones and posted them on the Internet and on social networking Web sites such as Twitter, Facebook, and YouTube. Some protestors called for a recount while Mousavi and others demanded a complete voiding of the election results. The government finally agreed to a partial recount, but on June 22, 2009, the Iranian Guardian Council, an agency charged with certifying elections in Iran, officially declared incumbent president Ahmadinejad winner and dismissed the challenges to the election results.

As spontaneous protests continued in late June and throughout the fall of 2009, the government repression worsened. According to human rights advocates, government police increased the number of arrests, began firing into the crowds of demonstrators, and also made nighttime raids on people's homes, trying to intimidate green activists in order to stop the movement. Many protestors were killed, including a young Iranian woman named Neda Agha-Soltan, who was filmed being shot by government troops and dying as she lay on an Iranian street. Neda soon became a martyr for the Green Movement, and her funeral became the spark for yet more demonstrations. Eventually, however, the government actions made it very risky for protesters to attend public demonstrations, and although the movement continues today underground, the protests have decreased in both number and size.

Many commentators have written that the goals of participants of the Green Movement are more democracy for Iran, expansion of human rights, and a secular government. These pro-democracy demonstrators are frustrated with the lack of personal freedoms under Iran's Islamic republic and object to Iran's state-run economy, which has produced double-digit unemployment in recent years. Mousavi and other Iranian politicians, who have been called the leaders of the Green

Movement, appear to be less radical than some of their followers. Mousavi has urged his supporters to refrain from calling for the overthrow of Iran's Islamic republic government or the death or dismissal of its supreme religious leader, Ayatollah Ali Khamenei. Long critical of the current regime, Mousavi still hopes to work within the existing system to achieve reform.

The future of the Green Movement is unclear at this juncture. Some observers suggest that President Ahmadinejad and Supreme Leader Khamenei will be able to smother the Green Movement, while others predict that the protestors will eventually either force significant reforms or bring down Iran's Islamic government. The viewpoints in this chapter discuss the strength of the Green Movement and its likelihood for success.

The Green Movement
Is Growing

Iason Athanasiadis and Barbara Slavin

Iason Athanasiadis is a reporter with the Washington Times, *an American newspaper. Barbara Slavin is an author and an assistant managing editor at the* Washington Times.

Iran's opposition movement has yet to produce a charismatic leader but has a diverse and growing group of organizers, including numerous students and veterans of an abortive 1999 uprising, Iran specialists say.

A New Generation of Activity

The Green Movement's titular heads remain Mir-Hossein Mousavi [Khameneh] and Mehdi Karroubi, the two presidential candidates who refused to accept the results of the June [2009] election that gave incumbent President Mahmoud Ahmadinejad a tainted "landslide" victory.

Government repression has limited their ability to move among the people. On Tuesday [December 29, 2009], Mr. Karroubi's son said authorities were no longer providing protection for his father when he leaves home, in effect putting him under house arrest. On Sunday, [December 27, 2009] a nephew of Mr. Mousavi was killed by security forces, according to opposition Web sites, to intimidate the candidate.

While the government focuses on these two men, however, a new generation of activists is working behind the scenes to sustain the movement's momentum.

"There appears to be a core of student leaders, recent graduates and people who were students in 1999," said Kenneth Katzman, an Iran specialist at the Congressional Research Service in Washington.

A new generation of activists is working behind the scenes to sustain the movement's momentum.

He said these leaders have "agreed on nonviolence and are trying to reach out to their parents' generation" and to supporters outside Iran.

Mr. Katzman said the activists had organized into cells of about 10 for security reasons.

"They are very optimistic," Mr. Katzman said. "They believe they are going to be rid of [the regime] in six months to a year. They feel that a lot of security people are starting to back off because they don't know how this will come out and don't want to be" on the losing side.

Students, Youth, and Others

Amir Abbas Fakhravar, 35, a former student leader who spent several years in prison in Iran and now lives in the Washington [D.C.] area, said contacts are taking place on Facebook and Skype and that activists plan to create a "revolutionary council" of about 15 people inside and outside Iran to lead the "Iranian Green Revolution." He said this leadership might emerge before Feb. 11 [2010], the 31st anniversary of the fall of Shah Mohammad Reza Pahlavi—another official holiday when masses of Iranians are likely to go into the streets to continue their protests.

Nader Uskowi, another Washington-based Iran specialist and consultant to the U.S. government, said, "We are probably a few months off from the day we see a clear leader emerging."

"The student organizations at major universities are still the most organized ones, but there are also other 'natural' organizations that appear nonpolitical but in fact are gathering places in which the news of planned actions and slogans are passed along, like associations of painters, calligraphers, etc.," he said.

"Students and youths are still the engine of the movement, but it is rapidly spreading to parents actively supporting their children."

Mr. Uskowi said the issue of leadership seems less urgent than the harder task of organizing a large organic movement. He said another strong incentive for leading personalities to keep a low profile is the regime's readiness to arrest anyone identified as an organizer.

Students and youths are still the engine of the movement, but it is rapidly spreading to parents actively supporting their children.

The Ministry of Intelligence has infiltrated agents into the Office for Consolidating Unity, a student body that led the last widespread student protests in 1999.

In July of that year, students at Tehran University gathered to protest the closure of a reform newspaper and were set upon by government-backed vigilantes known as Ansar e-Hezbollah. They threw students from dormitory balconies, killing at least one and injuring and arresting scores. Outraged, young people took to the streets of Tehran for a week, smashed store windows, threw stones at police and burned pictures of Ayatollah Ali Khamenei, Iran's supreme leader. Then President Mohammad Khatami, who initially supported the students, backed down under pressure from Ayatollah Khamenei and the Revolutionary Guard, and the movement fizzled.

Unlike the situation in 1999, however, the current movement has expanded far beyond university campuses to encompass disparate and overlapping groups, including human rights advocates, women, discontented clerics, unemployed and underemployed workers and directionless members of Iran's third post-revolutionary generation angry at the current order.

Clerical involvement, which had been relatively minor in the weeks and months after the June vote, has revived since the death Dec. 20 [2009] of Grand Ayatollah Ali Montazeri, a dissident once slated to be Iran's supreme leader. Government efforts to restrict mourning for the cleric brought thousands of angry, devout Shi'ites to the streets in the theological center of Qom and the cleric's hometown of Najafabad, which was put under martial law.

The . . . movement has expanded . . . to encompass disparate and overlapping groups, including human rights advocates, women, discontented clerics, unemployed and underemployed workers.

"Reformists organized the protests for Montazeri's death," said Roohollah Shahsavar, a youth activist in the northeastern Iranian city of Mashhad who escaped the country after consecutive arrests and now runs a newspaper called *Nedaye Sabz* (*Green Voice*) from his Paris exile. "The Green Revolution group is composed of reformist supporters of Khatami, Karroubi and Mousavi spread across Turkey, France and Belgium and also inside Iran," he said.

Seeking a Leader

Plenty of exiles are vying for control of the movement. Among them are Mr. Fakhravar and Reza Pahlavi, the son of the late shah [ruler of Iran].

On Thursday, Mr. Pahlavi urged nations worldwide to withdraw their ambassadors from Tehran. In an interview with the Associated Press, he equated the climate of the unrest in Iran now with the "revolutionary atmosphere" that preceded his father's overthrow. The difference, he said, is that this time the people know what they want—a secular democracy.

"Everyone wants to lead this movement but the question is whether the people out on the streets risking their own lives will accept self-styled leaders coming from Washington, Paris or even recent exiles in countries neighboring Iran," said Delbar Tavakoli, a journalist who was forced to flee to Ankara after the recent elections. "Even Mousavi and Karroubi have become a toy in the hands of the people—they don't have the latitude to issue anything beyond standard announcements or instruct supporters in how to behave."

A *Washington Times* reporter's experience in Iran immediately after the June elections gives a sense of how the protests are being organized.

A student leader in a bedroom in one of Tehran University's dormitories issued curt instructions into his cell phone to students in the streets.

"Let them burn rubbish bins but not any more banks," he said.

The spartan room was decorated with a potted cactus, a television monitor and a window whose glass had been smashed when a Basij paramilitary [part of Iran's military] had lobbed a stone through it during a raid the previous week.

"Mousavi supporters are nearing Tajrish now," a cell phone caller informed the student leader, illustrating how demonstrations were being organized at opposite sides of the city to stretch the capacity of police to respond.

The student leader was among hundreds of activists who have gone underground since the crisis began, hopping between the houses of sympathizers and emerging on demonstration days to organize resistance to the government.

Djavad Salehi-Esfahani, a professor of economics at Virginia Tech and an Iran specialist, said Mr. Mousavi, a former prime minister and revolutionary stalwart, still has the potential to lead the movement.

He "is doing well so far. I can't see him losing the leadership to others outside the country," Mr. Salehi-Esfahani said. "He has wide appeal and will probably have to fight elements inside the Green Movement who are pushing for overthrowing the Islamic republic rather than reforming it."

Mr. Katzman said, however, that many of the young people with whom he has had contact are not interested in the reformers. He said these young activists criticize foreign media for paying too much attention to Mr. Mousavi and Mr. Karroubi.

As violence escalates, the new leadership might be military, given the stake of the Revolutionary Guard in the status quo.

Whoever emerges, "the regime is definitely in trouble," Mr. Katzman said.

The Green Movement Could Fail for Lack of Leadership and Organization

Tara Mahtafar

Tara Mahtafar, a journalist, is currently the managing editor of PBS FRONTLINE's Tehran Bureau.

The unprecedented violence in Iran seen in the December 27 [2009] Ashura [a Muslim religious holiday] protests—which was committed by the regime and the opposition—showcased the emboldened opposition movement's capacity for civil disobedience as well as a decline in both the psychological and physical effectiveness of the regime's repressive security forces.

A Danger of Erosion

While nine protesters were slain and dozens injured, protesters managed to corner the black-clad anti-riot guards that Iranians call "Robocops," capture and disarm a number of security forces, knock Basij forces off motorbikes, and set fire to police vehicles. For many Iranians, Ashura marked a milestone in the opposition's tenacity and scale. However, the dynamics that have sustained the anti-government movement this far, although well-developed, have led to a glaring deficiency that is beginning to raise concerns.

The opposition, which relies on a decentralized grassroots network (both Web based and at a local level) for organization and communication, faces the danger of erosion once the current strategy of staging demonstrations on a preset "calendar" (December's Ashura, November's Students Day,

September's Jerusalem Day, and the upcoming 1979 revolution anniversary in February) runs out of dates. This is especially a problem, as isolated protests are unlikely to pressure Supreme Leader Ayatollah Ali Khamenei and the hard-line ruling bloc to back down. It is likely that if the opposition's campaign fails to yield a resolution by the one-year mark of the 2009 elections, the impetus to go on may peter out or the movement may abandon its principle of nonviolence and be driven underground and radicalized into armed struggle.

Ashura marked a milestone in the opposition's tenacity and scale.

A Lack of Leadership

A grave flaw weakening Iran's democratic movement today is a lack of concrete leadership. Mir-Hossein Mousavi [Khameneh], the movement's figurehead, is a very different leader from Ayatollah Ruhollah Khomeini [Iran's supreme leader from 1979–1989]—a fact that testifies to the increased political sophistication of Iranian society today. Mousavi is pushing for reform rather than revolution, and thus does not urge people to pour out into streets on a regular basis. Mousavi sells no ideology nor holds Khomeini's idol-like status and charisma among religious Iranians. While Khomeini sent messages to his public from the safety of Paris, Mousavi is under close surveillance in his Tehran [Iran's capital] home and in danger of being arrested.

Finally, Mousavi's role as leader is largely symbolic—a point he has often repeated in his seventeen formal declarations released to date. As early as June 20, Mousavi stated, "I believe that the motivation and creativity of people can pursue and attain your legitimate rights through new civil personalities. Stay assured that I will remain next to you," and, "The people's movement chose green as its symbol. I confess that in this, I followed them."

In another statement on September 5, Mousavi emphasized the responsibility that social networks must shoulder in propelling the movement forward: "Today, what plays the strongest role in our society is a capable and self-evolving social network that has stretched among a large group of people. . . . As a response to questions like what do we do, what I suggest is the consolidation of this social network."

A grave flaw weakening Iran's democratic movement today is a lack of concrete leadership.

Although some fault Mousavi's hands-off leadership style, most opposition supporters laud the critical function he has served: initiating public charges of electoral fraud, maintaining a firm commitment to standing up to the Khamenei-Ahmadinejad axis, widening the rift within the elite, and consolidating the opposition under the banner of the nonviolent, pro-democracy Green Movement. As its symbolic leader, Mousavi retains the authority to call mass demonstrations at will, if he chooses to call for more protests beyond the aforesaid strategic calendar. But in terms of delineating a blueprint for democratic transition, or of furthering the scope and efficiency of the movement, he is unable or unwilling to lead more actively at present.

A second weakness that Mousavi's role as sole leader poses for the movement is that his arrest would create a difficult-to-fill political void that could dampen the opposition's morale and slow down its progress.

The Need for a Coalition of Leadership

The grassroots network that the opposition has cultivated and is sustained by—a large part of which is Web based—provides a decentralized but ready platform for Iranians inside Iran to collaborate with the Iranian political community based abroad. Prominent public figures, such as Nobel laureate Shirin Ebadi and ex-Revolutionary Guard architect Mohsen Sazegara, who have been politically active in the post-election aftermath, as well as former Islamic republic parliamentarians and ministers and even dissident clerics, are in an unrestricted position to use this network to form a coalition of leadership based outside of Iran.

Such a coalition would not supplant Mousavi as de facto leader, but would supplement the effort spearheaded by reformist leaders (Mousavi, Mehdi Karroubi, and Mohammad Khatami) inside the country.

By projecting a unified voice that represents strong political clout and a democratic mission, this type of coalition could plug into the grassroots base of the movement in Iran and provide it with the centralized superstructure it currently lacks. By establishing a presence accessible via the Internet and satellite television, the coalition can introduce a higher level of organization to the beleaguered and fettered opposition.

Without presuming to "direct" the course of the movement (an act that would lend credence to the Iranian regime's accusations of plots to overthrow the system), the coalition's Web/satellite platform can supply a space for discourse to occur on vital issues that are not yet being addressed in any coherent way: the movement's core demands as well as goals and aspirations for the democratic Iran it is striving toward.

Panels and roundtables can bring Iranian economists, academics, and political analysts before the opposition audience to discuss various topics related to the ways in which Iran is currently being governed and executively managed. Experts can debate solutions to existing problems—including the nuclear conflict, economic policies, and relations with the region and the international community.

The vibrant opposition, mainly composed of Iran's majority youth and urban middle class, has proved its capacity in braving attacks, imprisonment, torture, and deaths, but lacks the resources and freedom for growth, organization, and development of clear goals and vision, due to the severe limitations within the country. The Iranian expatriate political community, however, can work together to establish an effective platform to serve this vital function.

The Leaders of the Green Movement Are Seeking Compromise, Not Victory

Keith Jones

Keith Jones is a writer for the World Socialist Web site, an online news source published by the world socialist movement.

All three of the principal leaders of Iran's "Green Revolution" bourgeois opposition have made conciliatory public statements in recent weeks [January 2010], backing off from their demand for the annulling of the June 2009 presidential election and reaffirming their support for the Islamic republic.

Statements of Compromise

Mir-Hossein Mousavi [Khameneh], who proclaimed himself—not the incumbent Mahmoud Ahmadinejad—the true victor of last June's presidential election, issued a statement at the beginning of the new year in which he denounced the government for repressing opposition protests on the Shia holy day of Ashura. The government's "policy of terror," said Mousavi, was causing some protesters to move "toward unacceptable radicalism" in their "slogans and actions."

But the former prime minister also called for "national unity," said he believes the current regime can be reformed, and suggested that the Ahmadinejad administration can be held to account by "the people, the parliament and judiciary" if political prisoners are released, bans on various pro-opposition newspapers are lifted, and the constitution's provisions concerning political activity are respected.

Mousavi also said that new election laws are needed so as to "regain the people's trust." But he did not advocate, in what he termed his "solution for getting out of the crisis," a fresh presidential election—hitherto his and the Green Movement's ostensible principal demand.

Shortly thereafter, Mohammad Khatami, Iran's president from 1997 to 2004 and one of the principal sponsors of Mousavi's election campaign, issued an even more conciliatory statement. "The reform movement and I personally," wrote Khatami, "recognize the current administration of Mr. Ahmadinejad, but we must combat extremism."

This past week [January 25, 2010], Mehdi Karroubi, a former speaker of Iran's parliament, a defeated candidate in the 2005 and 2009 presidential elections, and the third in the troika of Green leaders, issued a series of statements acknowledging Ahmadinejad as Iran's president and declaring the supreme leader or guardian of the Islamic republic, Ayatollah [Ali] Khamenei, the "best person" to solve the current political crisis.

Karroubi said slogans that called into question Khamenei's leadership, the post of supreme leader or *velayat-e faghih*, and other key institutions of the Islamic republic "are 100 percent wrong." "I don't agree with slogans that call for changing power structures."

He also condemned the right-wing, pro-US [United States] slogan taken up by opposition demonstrators on several occasions, most notably on Iran's traditional day of solidarity with the Palestinian people—"Neither Gaza, nor Lebanon. My life is for Iran."

Karroubi, it need be noted, had been until last week the most strident of the three Green leaders.

"There have been lots of efforts in the past few weeks to defuse the tension," an unnamed confidante of the opposition leaders told the *New York Times* late last month [January 2010].

The Green opposition has been hailed by all sections of the bourgeois political establishment in the US and Europe, including the nominal "left," as a "democratizing" movement. In fact it speaks for powerful elements within Iran's bourgeois-clerical establishment who bitterly oppose the populist policies that Ahmadinejad—who came to power as the result of a popular backlash against the neo-liberal policies implemented under Khatami and before him [Akbar] Hashemi Rafsanjani—pursued during his first term as president. They denounce Ahmadinejad for squandering the proceeds of the 2005–08 oil boom on price subsidies and social spending and for pursuing a needlessly confrontational policy toward the US. They also resent the growing economic and political power of the top brass of the Revolutionary Guard and its business cronies.

[The Green Movement's leaders] are concerned that the opposition protests . . . have assumed an increasingly radical character.

Reasons for Accommodation

Three interlinked factors account for the Green leaders' shift toward seeking an accommodation with Khamenei, even if it means accepting Ahmadinejad's presidency.

First, they are concerned that the opposition protests, which since their eruption last June have been dominated by middle-class layers, have assumed an increasingly radical character. Both openly right-wing, pro-monarchist and pro-US forces and self-avowed socialists have raised slogans calling into question the institutions of the Islamic republic.

Second, the world economic slump and US-led sanctions have dealt crippling blows to Iran's economy, driving up unemployment and inflation. Several of the country's largest banks are said to be in danger of default.

The Ahmadinejad government, with the full support of Khamenei, has responded to the crisis by shifting sharply to the right. It is vowing to press forward with privatization of much of the country's economy and has won parliamentary approval for a five-year scheme to phase out some $100 billion worth of subsides for gasoline, food, and other vital goods and services.

All sections of the Iranian elite recognize that these changes raise the prospect of an open confrontation with the working class and rural poor.

Last but not least, there is Washington's unrelenting campaign of pressure against Iran. While the Green Revolution leaders are amenable to a rapprochement with Washington, the US, under [President Barack] Obama, as previously under George W. Bush, has served notice that it will accept nothing less than unequivocal acceptance on Tehran's part of US hegemony in the Middle East. This has been exemplified by Washington's refusal to allow Iran to exercise its rights as a signatory to the Nuclear Non-Proliferation Treaty [Treaty on the Non-Proliferation of Nuclear Weapons] to develop a full-cycle civilian nuclear program.

The [Iranian] ... government, with the full support of [Supreme Leader Ali] Khamenei, has responded to the crisis by shifting sharply to the right.

In recent weeks the US and its European allies have ratcheted up their campaign of threats and bullying against Tehran, pledging that Iran's failure to agree to curbs on its civilian nuclear program will result in further economic sanctions.

Last week, the German industrial conglomerate Siemens [AG] announced that as of next summer it will seek no new orders in Iran. Siemens' announcement came the day after German Chancellor Angela Merkel told a joint press conference with Israeli President Shimon Peres that "Iran's time is up. It is now time to discuss widespread international sanctions."

In a voice vote last Thursday, the US Senate passed a bill calling for a gasoline export embargo on Iran that would be enforced by sanctions on foreign-based institutions that defy the US embargo. Such an embargo would have a huge impact since Iran, due to a lack of refining capacity, currently imports some 40 percent of its gasoline.

And on Friday, US newspapers reported that General [David] Petraeus, who oversees the US's wars in Iraq and Afghanistan, recently revealed that the US, with a view to a future conflict with Iran, has stationed anti-missile batteries in four Gulf States—Qatar, the United Arab Emirates, Bahrain and Kuwait—and will henceforth deploy Aegis anti-missile cruisers in the Persian Gulf at all times.

[Akbar] Hashemi Rafsanjani, a former president and current-day head of two of the Islamic republic's most important institutions—the Assembly of Experts and Expediency [Discernment] Council [of the System]—has over the past two months repeatedly pointed to the threat from the US in advocating a compromise between the Green opposition and the Ahmadinejad-Khamenei regime. Noting that "foreign enemies have a special account on the current dashes within the country," Rafsanjani recently declared, "now, more than any other time, unity among political forces of the country and people seems crucial."

Reputedly Iran's richest capitalist, Rafsanjani openly supported Mousavi's election campaign and his subsequent challenge to the legitimacy of Ahmadinejad's victory.

He is far from the only powerful voice within the current governing bodies of the Islamic republic to favor reconciliation between the rival factions of the clerical-bourgeois establishment.

Majlis Speaker Ali Larijani, who has close political and family ties to the top Shia clergy, has joined Rafsanjani in denouncing "extremism"—a term meant to denote both the more radical of the opposition protesters and those in the government who advocate increased repression.

In an effort to promote reconciliation, Iran's national television network last month broadcast several debates between prominent opposition and government supporters.

Support for Iran's Supreme Leader

However, there are powerful elements in the regime that remain opposed to any concessions to the opposition.

Ayatollah Mohammad Yazdi, a former head of Iran's judiciary and currently a member of Iran's Guardian Council or contitutional court, denounced Rafsanjani late last month for advocating compromise with those who "have separated themselves from" the supreme leader. "How," asked Yazdi, "can you say the moderates from both sides must resolve the issues with the leadership [Khamenei]? Tell us who the moderates of the opposition are."

Other government spokesmen have vowed that the opposition will not be allowed to use this month's commemorations of the February 11, 1979, revolution that toppled the brutal regime of the US-backed shah to mount protests. "Any voice or color other than the voice of the Islamic Revolution will be pushed aside," declared Brig. Gen. Hossein Hamedani, the Tehran Revolutionary Guard commander. "And if a minority makes such an attempt, it will be firmly confronted."

There are powerful elements in the regime that remain opposed to any concessions to the opposition.

Mousavi and Karroubi both condemned as "hasty" last week's hanging of two monarchists who had been found guilty of preparing terrorist attacks. While the two were arrested prior to last June's election, they were tried alongside Green Movement supporters.

An extensive interview Karroubi gave to the London-based *Financial Times* last week sheds further light on the orientation of the Green leaders.

He argued that the multiple crises enveloping the Islamic republic would propel "moderates" in both elite factions to unite so as to remove Ahmadinejad or at least sack many of his ministers and restrict his power and influence as president.

Said Karroubi, "I don't know how long it will take, but I think it won't take too long. Look at certain indices: inflation, stagnation of the economy, closure of economic centers, in particular industrial units, which are working with 20 or 40 per cent of their capacities, increasing unemployment, poverty line standing at 7m rials ($700) which means above 40 per cent of people are poor."

Karroubi emphasized his support for the Islamic republic, including the institution of *velayat-e faqih*, which underpins the exalted political position of the Shia clergy within the Islamic republic. But in so doing, he also revealed his fear of a revolutionary challenge to the regime from the working class.

"A majority of people," Karroubi told the *Financial Times*, "do not want to overthrow the regime. In fact, anyone who cares about the future of this country is not after toppling the regime because it is not clear what would come out of it. If it was not thanks to the extraordinary leadership skills of Imam [Ayatollah Ruhollah] Khomeini, God knows what would have happened to Iran with the 1979 revolution."

What Karroubi is referring to is the pivotal role Ayatollah Khomenei played in harnessing, through Shia populism, the popular anti-imperialist upsurge that convulsed Iran between 1978 and 1982 to the program of the bourgeoisie, while deploying the state apparatus—with the full support of Mousavi, Rafsanjani and Khamenei—to ruthlessly suppress the left and all independent working-class organizations.

The Green Movement Is a Viable Civil Rights Movement

Hooman Majd

Hooman Majd is a writer based in New York who has advised and interpreted for two Iranian presidents, Mohammad Khatami and Mahmoud Ahmadinejad, on their trips to the United States.

"The Green Movement Is Winning." Yes, but over time. The answer depends on what "winning" means. One thing Western observers should have learned from 30 years of second-guessing Iran and Iranians is that second-guessing Iran and Iranians is often a mistake, and predicting the imminent demise of the Islamic theocracy is unrealistic.

A Civil Rights Movement

What is evident is that if we consider Iran's pro-democracy "green movement" not as a revolution but as a civil rights movement—as the leaders of the movement do—then a "win" must be measured over time. The movement's aim is not for a sudden and complete overthrow of Iran's political system. That may disappoint both extremes of the American and Iranian political spectrums, left and right, and especially U.S. neoconservatives hoping for regime change.

Seen in this light, it's evident that the green movement has already "won" in many respects, if a win means that many Iranians are no longer resigned to the undemocratic aspects of a political system that has in the last three decades regressed rather than progressed, in affording its citizens the rights promised to them under Iran's own constitution.

The Islamic republic's fractured leadership recognizes this, as is evident in its schizophrenic reaction to events since the disputed June [2009] election. Although the hard-liners in power may be able to suppress general unrest by sheer force, the leadership is also aware that elections in the Islamic state can never be held as they were in 2009 (even conservatives have called for a more transparent electoral system), nor can the authorities completely silence opposition politicians and their supporters or ignore their demands over the long term.

It augurs well for eventual democratic reform in Iran that the green movement continues to exist at all. Despite all efforts by the authorities to portray it as a dangerous counterrevolution, the green movement continues to attract supporters and sympathizers from even the clergy and conservative Iranians.

The green movement morphed from a political campaign into a campaign to annul the presidential election—and then, more broadly, into a movement to restore . . . civil liberties.

Peaceful Reform

"The Green Movement Is Radicalizing." Only in part. It's important to remember that Iran's green movement began well before protests broke out in June 2009. The origins were in the *mowj-e-sabz*, also known as the "green wave," a campaign to support the presidential bid of reformist candidate Mir-Hossein Mousavi [Khameneh], who ran against conservative incumbent Mahmoud Ahmadinejad.

The green wave's goals were to wrest the presidency and executive power away from radical hard-liners whose term in office had been marked by economic incompetence, foreign policy adventurism, and an ideological doctrine that included new limits on civil rights and that Mousavi's supporters believed was unsuited to Iranian interests in the 21st century.

After the disputed election results, the green movement morphed from a political campaign into a campaign to annul the presidential election—and then, more broadly, into a movement to restore the civil liberties promised by the 1979 Islamic Revolution. With every instance of recent government tyranny, from show trials of opposition politicians and journalists to the beatings and murders of some demonstrators on Iran's streets, the movement has grown more steadfast in its demands for the rights of the people.

Over time, and particularly with the government's continued use of brutal force against its citizens, some Iranians are no longer satisfied with the stated goals of the green movement, but are looking to topple the Islamic regime altogether. For instance, we hear in the Western media many instances of Iranians clamoring for an "Iranian," rather than Islamic, republic or for "death to the supreme leader." Meanwhile we see on YouTube and our TVs footage of Iranians violently confronting security forces.

However, the radical elements claiming to be a part of the green movement only speak for a small minority of Iranians. The majority still want peaceful reform of the system and not necessarily a wholesale revolution, bloody or otherwise. That's why, in the most recent Ashura [a Muslim holiday] demonstrations, for example, large groups of peaceful marchers actually prevented some of the movement's radicalized elements from beating or attacking security forces. Although accurate polling information is not available, based on what we hear and see of the leaders of the green movement and many of its supporters, radicalization is still limited to a minority of protesters.

The green movement's leaders recognize that any radicalization on their part will only bring down the state's iron fist. They are also cautious because they know that if movement leaders call for regime change rather than reform and adherence to the constitution, they will only have proven the government's assertion that the movement's goal all along has been to topple the system.

The View of the Revolutionary Guard

"The Revolutionary Guard [a branch of Iran's military] Will Do Anything to Keep Khamenei in Power." Don't bet on it. The Revolutionary Guard is tasked with protecting the legacy of the 1979 Islamic Revolution and its embodiment in the *velayat-e-faqih*, the supreme leader, currently Ayatollah Ali Khamenei.

The radical elements claiming to be a part of the green movement only speak for a small minority of Iranians. The majority still want peaceful reform.

The Guard's top leaders are military men who have served many years in the ranks and as such are unlikely to disobey the orders of their commander in chief. Their view, as they have expressed repeatedly in public fora, is that the green movement and its leaders are a threat to the revolution and to the supreme leader. But they are probably more concerned with protecting the *position* of the leader (and their own power and pervasive influence in Iranian business and politics) than they are in protecting a particular individual.

There are many former top commanders of the Guard, such as Mohsen Rezai (a defeated candidate in the presidential election), Mohammad Qalibaf (Tehran's popular mayor), and Ali Larijani (speaker of the parliament), who oppose [Iranian President Madmoud] Ahmadinejad (and have influence with the Guard), but have not so far challenged the supreme leader. That doesn't mean, though, that they would not look to replace [Supreme Leader Ali] Khamenei should it become apparent that he is an obstacle to the regime's stability. Although any moves against the supreme leader are highly unlikely at this point (and he still has the support of the majority of the members of the Assembly of Experts, the body that elects, monitors, and can even impeach him), that doesn't mean that such a challenge could never happen.

Potential for Compromise

"The Time for Compromise Is Over." Not in Iran, it ain't. The supreme leader, the Revolutionary Guard, and almost all of the hard-liners in government have said that they will tolerate no more dissent; they have said that there will be no compromise and that the green movement's demands will not be met. But that doesn't actually mean that some form of compromise isn't possible.

For starters, the green movement's leaders may recognize that they could become irrelevant if they are unwilling to either become more revolutionary (as some of their supporters already have), or compromise to protect the longevity of their movement as a civil rights campaign.

On Jan. 1 [2010], Mousavi listed the green movement's demands on civil rights and other reforms, but significantly he was no longer calling for an annulment of the 2009 election. Meanwhile, at the most recent meeting of the Expediency [Discernment] Council [of the System], the body that arbitrates disputes between Iran's executive and legislative branches, Mohsen Rezai, the conservative challenger to Ahmadinejad in the 2009 election, suggested that the government should listen to Mousavi's demands, describing them as "constructive."

Both sides realize that the continuing unrest threatens the country's stability and that neither side is looking to reform the regime into oblivion. The current standoff makes no one happy. The odds aren't horrible that some form of compromise might occur in 2010, a compromise that would allow both sides to claim advances if not outright victory.

No Need for Foreign Support

"The Green Movement Wants or Needs Foreign Support." Dead wrong. Nothing could be further from the truth. It is insulting and patronizing to suggest, as many commentators do, that without foreign help or support the green movement cannot be successful, that Iranians on their own are incapable of commanding their own destiny.

U.S. President Barack Obama has so far expressed only moral support for Iranians fighting for their civil rights and has rightly articulated the unrest in Iran as a purely Iranian affair. Lacking relations with Iran, Obama can do little to help the green movement, but plenty to hurt it. Coming out squarely on the side of the opposition in Iran is likely to undermine its credibility, and perhaps even lend credence to the government's assertion that the movement is a foreign-inspired plot that will rob Iran of its independence.

That the green movement has survived, and even grown, in the absence of foreign support is evidence that Iranians are perfectly capable of maintaining a civil rights movement and agitating for democratic change without the prodding, influence, or support of foreigners. Furthermore, if there is only one aspect of the Islamic Revolution that almost all Iranians can agree on as positive, it's that key events, such as the spontaneous unrest after the election and all the way back to the revolution itself, have happened independent of foreign influence.

The green movement is most definitely real, cannot be completely suppressed, and will undoubtedly have a long-term effect on the politics of the Islamic republic.

The most potentially damaging accusation the government has made against the green movement is that it is a foreign plot to foment a "velvet" or "color" revolution that will once again render Iran subservient to a greater power. But this accusation has not stuck because the movement's leaders have always eschewed any foreign support and framed their fight as a purely Iranian one.

The idea that foreign support is either necessary or important to the green movement's ability to achieve its goals is as preposterous as imagining, say in 1965, that overt Soviet support of the civil rights movement in the United States was necessary for that movement to be successful.

For observers sitting in the United States or anywhere outside Iran, it is tempting to draw conclusions about the green movement or even the health of the Islamic regime based on what little information we are able to gather and what various analysts believe, given the extreme restrictions Iran has placed on journalists and reporting from Iran. However, Iran often defies expectations and has proven maddeningly immune from adhering to conventional wisdom. Listen to an Iranian exile opposed to the Islamic regime for five minutes and you'll be convinced that the regime's days are numbered not in years, but in months. Listen to a regime apologist for five minutes and you might be persuaded that Western powers are indeed fomenting the revolt and that the government will weather the storm and emerge as powerful as ever.

The truth, of course, always lies somewhere in between. The green movement is most definitely real, cannot be completely suppressed, and will undoubtedly have a long-term effect on the politics of the Islamic republic. What began with the election of reformist President Mohammad Khatami in 1997 has finally culminated in a civil rights movement that by any name will continue to put pressure on the regime to reform, pressure that it can only ignore at the peril of its own demise.

Iran Is Turning into a Military Dictatorship

Michael Petrou

Michael Petrou is a reporter for Maclean's, *a Canadian weekly newsmagazine.*

In the four months since Iranian President Mahmoud Ahmadinejad stole the June 12 [2009] presidential election, thousands of Iranian opposition supporters have disappeared into the maw of Iranian prisons, where many have been beaten and raped. Among these uncounted victims, the detention of three young brothers is particularly significant. Mohammad Mahdi Montazeri, [Mohammad] Sadegh Montazeri, and Mohammad Ali Montazeri were detained in the holy city of Qom last month [September 2009]. None is said to be politically active. But they are all grandsons of Grand Ayatollah Hossein Ali Montazeri.

Hossein Ali Montazeri, 87, was a leader of the Iranian Revolution of 1979, and was once the designated successor to the Islamic republic's founding supreme leader, Ayatollah Ruhollah Khomeini. Montazeri clashed with Khomeini in 1989 over abuses committed by the government, particularly the execution of the 13-year-old daughter of a colleague who was suspected of belonging to an opposition group. He's been a firm government critic ever since, but has remained politically powerful. Despite a period of house arrest from 1997 to 2003, his influence and prestige among Iran's most senior clerics afforded him some protection.

That protection vanished this summer. "No one in their right mind can believe" the official election results, Montazeri said of Ahmadinejad's apparent victory. When protests were crushed, Montazeri warned soldiers and police that "receiving orders will not excuse them before God." He called for three days of public mourning after female protester Neda Agha-Soltan was shot by a sniper. And he condemned the silence of other clerics in the face of these abuses against Iran's own citizens. Reasoning that targeting Montazeri directly would not shut him up, the regime went after his family.

Relatives of other dissident clerics have also been jailed. These are men who only months ago were part of Iran's establishment—were Ahmadinejad's challengers for the presidency, Mehdi Karroubi and Mir-Hossein Mousavi [Khameneh]. The fact that they are now treated as political subversives reflects the enormous changes that are taking place within Iran's power structure. One Iranian exile described it, with only a hint of sardonic exaggeration, as regime change, but not the regime change that George W. Bush had hoped for. Religious and political leaders who question Ahmadinejad's right to govern risk seeing their grandsons hauled away. A country that was once a theocracy with multiple pillars of power is transforming into a more familiar military dictatorship, where power is increasingly concentrated in the hands of the Revolutionary Guard and the pro-government Basij militia.

A country that was once a theocracy with multiple pillars of power is transforming into a more familiar military dictatorship.

A Missed Opportunity for the United States

There are different ways to interpret these changes. To be sure, they are worrying. The Revolutionary Guards are violent, radical, and unaccountable. But they are also widely scorned within Iran, and their ascent and aggression reflects both the fragility of and the lack of popular legitimacy for Ahmadinejad's renewed presidency.

This raises the question of how the United States and its allies should deal with Iran. U.S. President Barack Obama came to office promising to engage with the country over its nuclear program, and he has. Talks in Geneva [Switzerland] this month [October 2009] between Iran and six of the world's leading powers (France, Britain, the United States, Russia, China, and Germany) resulted in Iran agreeing to allow international inspectors to visit a newly revealed nuclear plant in Qom. It's unclear whether this represents a genuine Iranian change of heart or if it is simply a stalling tactic to avoid sanctions.

What has been largely overlooked, however, is the possibility that, by focusing on Iran's nuclear program, the United States has confronted Ahmadinejad on ground where he is most comfortable making a stand, and it has missed an opportunity to challenge the Iranian president on issues where he is most vulnerable—the legitimacy of his rule and the rights of his fellow citizens.

The argument that Iran's nuclear program is a misplaced priority for the United States is based on an unpalatable assumption that is nevertheless likely true: that Iran will eventually develop a nuclear weapon—or at least the capability to do so. Negotiated deals, sanctions, even military strikes might disrupt Iran's nuclear program, but they are unlikely to end it. "The most important part of the program is human capital— the scientists and engineers. And they're still going to be there," says Daniel Byman, director of Georgetown University's Center for Peace and Security Studies.

According to Payam Akhavan, a professor of international law at McGill University, "The international community could possibly delay Iran's acquisition of nuclear capability but it cannot stop it. Sooner or later, Iran, which has a highly educated population, will acquire nuclear capability. That's an unavoidable fact," he said in an interview with *Maclean's*. "But at the end of the day, the problem is with the regime and not with its nuclear capability. There are many countries with nuclear capability: Japan, Brazil, Argentina, South Africa, and Korea. We don't worry about those regimes, largely because they are democratic. A regime that is democratic is going to respond to the real demands of the people, which are economic and democratic issues. A regime that uses violence against its own citizens is more likely to use violence as a means of extending influence against its neighbours."

The United States has . . . missed an opportunity to challenge the Iranian president on issues where he is most vulnerable—the legitimacy of his rule and the rights of his fellow citizens.

Nuclear Power as a Rally Point

Fair enough, President Obama or French President Nicolas Sarkozy might say. We wish Iran were democratic, too. But it's not. And in the meantime Iran's nuclear program is not something we can safely ignore.

This is true. According to Byman, it is unlikely that Iran would launch an unprovoked strike against Israel or the United States, or that it would give nuclear technology to a terrorist group. But the repercussions would still be severe. With a nuclear umbrella protecting it, Iran would be emboldened to extend its influence in Afghanistan and Iraq, and through its proxies Hamas [a Palestinian political and paramilitary movement] and Hezbollah [a political and paramilitary movement based in Lebanon], in the Levant [the Eastern Mediterranean]. Iran's neighbours and adversaries in the Middle East, particularly Egypt, Saudi Arabia, and Turkey, would feel threatened and might reason that they too must acquire nuclear weapons to protect themselves. So even if Iran's nuclear program can only be stalled, the ramifications of a nuclear Iran are sufficiently dire that playing for time is a better option than doing nothing.

But those countries negotiating with Iran should also consider that the nuclear issue is a powerful propaganda tool for Iranian hard-liners at a moment when the Islamic regime is weaker than it has been for decades. "The nuclear issue has been presented to the Iranian public as the right of Iran to develop nuclear technology for peaceful purposes. And Western attempts to prevent Iran from acquiring that capability have been portrayed as attacks on Iran's sovereignty and attempts to keep Iran backwards and dependent on the West," says Akhavan. "Iranians have a strong sense of national identity. They have memories of imperial domination by the British and the Russians, and of America's role in the 1953 *coup d'état* against [former prime minister Mohammad] Mosaddeq. The regime is playing to that sentiment."

The Islamic republic, in short, is in turmoil.

It's a public relations ploy with limited appeal. Saeed Rahnema, a professor of political science at York University, says that most Iranians are concerned about political freedoms, education, and economic opportunities rather than Iran's nuclear capability—an assessment that is echoed by Arash Azizi, an Iranian journalist who recently immigrated to Canada. Still, according to Djavad Salehi-Isfahani, a research fellow at Harvard University's Belfer Center for Science and International Affairs, "Iranians generally rally to the side of the government when the United States and the French say unreasonable things. And most Iranians know that what Iran is doing, Brazil is doing as well."

None of this is to suggest that Iran's nuclear program isn't important—only that it is not the most important thing happening in Iran right now. What will ultimately matter more to Iran's future, and the future of Iran's relationship with the rest of the world, is the fracturing of Iran's power structure, the emergence of the Revolutionary Guard as the dominant pro-government force in the country, and the continued resilience of Iran's democratic opposition.

The Islamic republic, in short, is in turmoil. And where it can be most effectively challenged is not over nuclear weapons but its democratic legitimacy and the rights of its citizens. These are issues on which the United States and its Western allies can assert their values and count on a greater degree of support from Iranian citizens themselves.

"There should always be room for dialogue, but I think that when the nuclear issue becomes the focal point, that is a mistake," says Akhavan. He notes that international travel bans and asset freezes have been directed against individuals and institutions linked to Iran's nuclear program, not to the ongoing human rights abuses that matter much more to people inside Iran. "People are saying, 'What about crimes against humanity? What about leaders that are responsible for murders and torture and rape? Why do we not have targeted sanctions against them? Why is everyone worried about the nuclear issue and the question of oil supplies, but nobody is worried about our struggle?'"

The Green Movement Is a Revolution That Will Ultimately Succeed

Amir Fakhravar

Amir Fakhravar serves as the secretary general of the Confederation of Iranian Students in Washington, D.C.

It has taken seven months and countless victims for the word "revolution" to be used to describe the protests in Iran. Why? There has been a tireless campaign, including by some Iranians outside Iran, to reduce the Green Movement to a call for "reforms" that keep the current government in place, with a few changes here and there.

Not so. What we are witnessing on the streets of Tehran [Iran's capital] and other cities is nothing short of a revolution—a carefully orchestrated, years-in-the-making attempt to overthrow a corrupt and repressive regime and replace it with something fundamentally more free, democratic and secular.

A Strong, Effective Movement

Watching the events unfold, I am taken back 15 years, when I was a student activist in medical school. In my first speech on campus, on Jan. 7, 1994, I simply said that in our country we don't have freedom the way the supreme leader says we do.

For saying this, I was sentenced to three years in prison. None of my schoolmates dared talk to me anymore; a combination of fear and religious beliefs had made even thinking ill of Ayatollah Ali Khamenei a taboo.

Today, when I see Iranians fearlessly shouting "Death to Khamenei" and "Khamenei is a murderer" with police and members of the Basij militia present, I know that the Green Revolution has found its correct course.

In my first speech on campus, on Jan. 7, 1994, I simply said that in our country we don't have freedom the way the supreme leader says we do.

I know it is strong enough not only to survive, but to succeed.

Iranians have come a long way to arrive at this moment. More than 70% of the population is younger than 30; young people's disappointment with previous empty promises of reform led to the student uprising of July 9, 1999—beginning to transform appeals for reform into more profound calls for democracy.

After those protests, we were arrested, tortured and sentenced to years in prison. But the struggle continued, and other young people learned from our experiences. Four years ago, after large-scale fraud in the elections that resulted in the presidency of Mahmoud Ahmadinejad—and the extremist stances of his government—Iranians grew even more frustrated.

Anger escalated. Protests grew louder. Young Iranians began using Facebook and Twitter to organize themselves. Months before the 2009 presidential elections, they decided to use the mullahs' own tactics against them—and to seize and own all of the icons of the Islamic republic and give them a new identity.

For example, though most of the protesters are secular, they chose green, the symbolic color of Shiite Islam, as the color of their movement. It was clever. It was savvy. It was effective.

So when there was massive fraud in Ahmadinejad's reelection, the people were ready. The Green Movement occupied the streets until Khamenei ordered a clampdown. The next day, Neda [Agha-Soltan]—the woman who bled in the street in that infamous video [of her killing posted on the Internet]—and other young greens were killed.

The planning of all those years planted the seeds; the brutality provided the spark. The Green Movement finally gained a complete identity with powerful symbols—even with its own martyrs.

On Quds Day [a holiday celebrating Muslim solidarity with Palestinians], chants of "Death to Israel" turned into "Neither Gaza nor Lebanon, I will give my life for Iran." On the anniversary of the hostage-taking at the American Embassy, "Death to America" became "Death to Russia."

Young people's disappointment with previous empty promises of reform led to the student uprising of July 9, 1999—beginning to transform appeals for reform into more profound calls for democracy.

A Matter of Time

The only question now is how long it will take. Three elements can affect this time line. The first is Iranians inside Iran, who are already doing their part. The second is a coalition including different Iranian opposition groups to synchronize future protests and help shape the foundations of a new democratic and secular government upon the downfall of the Islamic republic. The third is Western governments, who must impose hard sanctions on the regime to dramatically reduce the inflow of money, thus freeing the region and the world of a tyrannical and dangerous government.

CHAPTER 4

What Approach Should the United States Take Toward Iran?

Chapter Preface

Although the relationship between the United States and Iran today is difficult, Iran once had a pro-Western government that maintained good relations with the United States for many decades. This friendly U.S./Iran period began in 1941, when Prince Mohammad Reza Pahlavi replaced his father as shah, or king, of Iran. During World War II, Iran helped the British and the United States supply aid to Russia, an Allied power. Later in 1953, the United States and Britain supported and funded a coup against Mohammad Mossadeq, a popular Iranian prime minister who sought to give the Iranian government control over Iran's oil industry—a move that would have damaged Britain's oil interests in the region. After a period of crisis during which the shah was forced to flee Iran, the coup restored him to power. Over the next several decades, the United States provided millions of dollars of financial and military support for the shah, helping him to modernize Iran, boost its oil production and its economy, and improve health and education for the Iranian people. This U.S. support continued even as the shah's government became increasingly repressive throughout the 1960s and 1970s. The U.S. motive was to stabilize Iran and prevent it from becoming an ally of the Communists during the Cold War—a period of political tension and military rivalry between the Soviet Union and the United States that began after World War II and ended in 1991 with the economic and political collapse of the Soviet Union.

U.S. support for Iran abruptly stopped, however, in 1979, with the Iranian Revolution—a political transformation led by a religious leader, Ayatollah Ruhollah Khomeini, which succeeded in overthrowing the shah and establishing an Islamic republic in Iran. During the revolution, on November 4, 1979, anti-American, radical Islamist students in Iran seized the

American embassy, taking fifty-three Americans as hostages and holding them for 444 days. An attempt to rescue the hostages, authorized by then U.S. president Jimmy Carter, failed and helped to ensure Carter's defeat and the election of Ronald Reagan as president in 1980. The hostage crisis made it clear that Iran was no longer an American ally, and the incident was the beginning of a decades-long period of hostility between the two countries. There have been no diplomatic relations between the United States and Iran since 1979.

U.S.-Iran relations soured further when the Reagan administration backed Iraq after it invaded Iran in 1980. U.S. officials hoped that supporting Iraq would help to control the spread of radical Islam in Iran and other places in the Middle East. The ensuing eight-year Iran-Iraq war resulted in the death of tens of thousands of both Iraqis and Iranians and fanned anti-American sentiment in Iran. In 1988, Iranians found yet another reason to dislike the United States when a U.S. warship, the USS *Vincennes*, accidentally shot down an Iranian commercial airplane, killing all 290 civilians on board. Relations deteriorated again during the administration of President Bill Clinton, who imposed oil and trade sanctions on Iran for sponsoring terrorism in the Middle East and for secretly seeking to acquire nuclear weapons. Concern about development of Iran's nuclear weapons and its support of radical Islamist groups in Lebanon and elsewhere also caused President George W. Bush in 2002 to call Iran part of an "axis of evil" along with Iraq and North Korea. An international standoff over Iran's nuclear program culminated in the fall of 2003, when Iran agreed to suspend its uranium enrichment program and allow tougher United Nations inspections of its nuclear facilities.

Today, the dispute between the United States and Iran over its nuclear program continues. Iran openly develops nuclear power and claims it is for peaceful energy purposes, but many political observers worry that Iran really wants nuclear weapons capability to enhance its security and power in a volatile Middle East region. Since Iraq has often acted as the counterbalance to Iranian military power, U.S. officials are also concerned about what will happen in the future since the United States has now pulled its forces out of Iraq. Furthermore, Israel, a staunch U.S. ally in the region, fears that an Iran with nuclear weapons would be an unacceptable threat to its national security. The question of what approach the United States should take toward Iran in light of these various concerns is the subject of this chapter.

The United States Must Seek Tougher Sanctions Against Iran

Morton M. Kondracke

Morton M. Kondracke is an American political commentator and journalist who currently serves as executive editor and columnist for the nonpartisan Capitol Hill newspaper Roll Call.

Just how seriously does the White House take the threat of Iran's nuclear program? It's hard to tell.

In his 71-minute State of the Union address last week, President Obama devoted just five lines to what may emerge as the top foreign policy issue of 2010.

"The international community is more united, and the Islamic Republic of Iran is more isolated," he said.

"And, as Iran's leaders continue to ignore their obligations, there should be no doubt: They . . . will face growing consequences. That is a promise."

The good news comes with the word "as." It replaces the previous "if," indicating that Obama has finally concluded that diplomacy is failing to stop Iran's work on a bomb and that it's time to move to "consequences."

Secretary of State Hillary Rodham Clinton says the administration will now, finally, seek international agreement on "crippling sanctions" against Iran, but the process is going to be slow and there's reason to doubt that the Iranian regime really will be crippled.

Congress, to its credit, is far ahead of the administration. In December, the House passed, 412–12, the Iran Refined Petroleum Sanctions Act, authorizing steps to cut off Iran's imports of gasoline.

Last week, the Senate passed a similar bill on a voice vote with no dissent. Though Iran is oil-rich, it lacks refining capacity and has to import 40 percent of its gasoline. When the government rationed gas in 2006, riots ensued.

In a speech Jan. 24, House Foreign Affairs Chairman Howard L. Berman (D-Calif.), chief sponsor of the House measure, declared, "In my view, there is no greater threat to the world than the prospect of a nuclear Iran."

You don't hear that kind of talk from the administration—and, according [to] Rep. Mark Steven Kirk (R-Ill.), original sponsor of the gasoline-cutoff legislation in 2006, the administration seems reluctant to impose any sanctions that might adversely affect the Iranian people.

Adm. Dennis Blair, the administration's director of national intelligence, buried Iran deep in his annual worldwide threat assessment this week.

And he pointedly did not reverse a 2007 National Intelligence Estimate—reportedly disputed by both foreign and U.S. intelligence agencies—that Iran stopped its nuclear weaponization program in 2003.

"We continue to assess [that] Iran is keeping open the option to develop nuclear weapons in part by developing various nuclear capabilities that bring it closer to being able to produce such weapons, should it choose to do so," he told the Senate Intelligence Committee. "We do not know, however, if Iran will eventually decide to build nuclear weapons."

As all the world knows, Iran has been secretly enriching uranium, defying international demands that it stop, building missiles capable of carrying warheads and threatening the existence of Israel.

According to some press reports, it is also working on a sophisticated nuclear detonation system.

The Obama administration set a deadline for the end of last year for Iran to respond to its diplomatic "outreach." The deadline passed a month ago.

The next step is to seek tougher sanctions at the UN Security Council this month. But that's almost certain to fail because China will veto them.

Iranian President Mahmoud Ahmadinejad just gave China a perfect excuse to do so by saying he sees "no problem" with agreeing to a proposal to ship uranium out of the country for reprocessing.

Iran previously has rejected that idea. Hinting it might accept it is clearly designed to ward off sanctions and play for time.

The next step, if the administration is serious, would be to form a "coalition of the willing" with Europe to impose tough economic sanctions.

Iran has been secretly enriching uranium, defying international demands that it stop, building missiles capable of carrying warheads and threatening the existence of Israel.

One talked-of action is an international economic boycott of entities connected with the Iran Revolutionary Guard Corps, the powerful political-military-clerical conglomerate that now controls the country, including much of its energy and nuclear program.

Another is isolation of Iran's central bank from international commerce, which could collapse the value of Iran's currency.

On its own, the United States could enforce the 1996 Iran Sanctions Act, which calls for exclusion from U.S. business of any company in the world doing more than $20 million worth of business with Iran's energy sector.

No penalties have ever been imposed under the law—despite the fact that Iran just signed a $1.4 billion natural gas deal with an unnamed German firm, widely believed to be Siemens AG.

Last week, Siemens announced it would stop doing business with Iran—but not until the middle of this year.

Sanctions on Iran Will Only Hurt Ordinary Iranians

Muhammad Sahimi

Muhammad Sahimi is a professor of chemical engineering and materials science and a professor of petroleum engineering at the University of Southern California. He has written extensively about Iran's nuclear program.

On Thursday, January 28 [2010], the Senate approved legislation that allows the president to impose sanctions on any entity that exports gasoline to Iran, or help expand its refining capacity by denying them loans from American financial institutions. A largely similar legislation has already been passed by the House of Representatives. The legislation is supposedly intended to pressure the Islamic Republic [of Iran] to give up its uranium enrichment program.

The Senate bill extends sanctions to companies that build oil and gas pipelines in Iran and provide tankers to move Iran's petroleum. It also prohibits the U.S. government from buying goods from foreign companies that work in Iran's energy sector. So, in effect the Senate bill imposes sanctions on Iran's entire oil and natural gas industry.

Iran has the world's third biggest oil reserves, but imports a significant fraction of its gasoline to meet domestic demand, because it lacks enough refining capacity. Anticipating the gasoline sanctions for at least two years, Iran has been working hard to reduce its dependency on imports of gasoline, reducing it from 40 percent of total consumption to 25–30 percent. In addition, . . . Tehran [capital of Iran] can take several relatively simple steps to further reduce its dependency on the gasoline imports.

The Administration's Position

Although in his State of the Union address on Wednesday January 27, President [Barack] Obama warned Iran that it faces "growing consequences" over its nuclear program, the administration was not overly interested in the legislation. On January 4, Secretary of State Hillary Clinton stated that:

"Our goal is to pressure the Iranian government, particularly the Revolutionary Guard [Islamic Revolutionary Guard Crops, or IRGC] elements, *without contributing to the suffering of the ordinary [Iranians], who deserve better than what they currently are receiving.*"

This is a position that she reiterated on January 11.

P.J. Crowley, the State Department spokesman, reiterated the administration position on January 5:

"As the secretary said, one possibility is to focus more specifically on the Revolutionary Guard, the IRGC. We're taking a much more prominent role within Iran. We want to do this in a way that can *target specific entities within the Iranian government but not punish the Iranian people,* who are clearly looking for a different relationship with their government."

The [sanctions] legislation is terrible news for ordinary Iranians that have been struggling to make ends meet, amidst the deep [political] crisis that their nation has been facing.

Thus, the administration is apparently seeking targeted sanctions that hurt only the Islamic Revolutionary Guard Corps (IRGC), the elite hard-line part of Iran's military that essentially runs the country. Clearly, gasoline sanctions is not one of them. The U.S. business groups had also warned the administration that the bill would undercut the president's strategy of working with U.S. allies in finding a diplomatic solution to Iran's nuclear program, because the legislation targets the U.S. allies' companies that do business with Iran.

But, the Israel lobby and its agents in the Senate, Senator Joseph Lieberman and others, wanted the legislation approved, and so it was. Indeed, the passage of the legislation was praised by the American Israel Public Affairs Committee, which called for even tougher sanctions.

Sanctions Terrible for Ordinary Iranians

The legislation is terrible news for ordinary Iranians that have been struggling to make ends meet, amidst the deep crisis that their nation has been facing in the aftermath of the June 12 [2009] rigged presidential election. At least a million Iranians work in the transportation sector of Iran's economy, with millions more depending on transportation for their work and business, not to mention the agriculture sector that also relies heavily on transportation.

In addition, it is well known in Iran that there is a gasoline "Mafia" that is linked to the IRGC. They sell the gasoline that is subsidized by the government in neighboring countries at a much higher price and make a huge profit. The sanctions, which inevitably would lead to much higher gasoline price in Iran, would only tighten the "Mafia's" grip on the gasoline market, hence increasing the power that the IRGC already has, completely the opposite of the effect that the legislation is supposedly intended for.

If the purpose of such legislation is to create hardship for Iranians in order to motivate them to put pressure on their government, there is no need for it. A great majority of Iranians are already deeply angered about what has been happening in Iran in the aftermath of the June 12 rigged presidential election. There have been almost constant demonstrations; daily arrests of political figures, journalists, university students, human rights advocates and ordinary people; thousands have been detained; dozens have been murdered; show trials have been held; unjustified sentences have been handed out to the imprisoned people; and several have been hanged.

These developments have given birth to the Green Movement that has been gathering strength over the past several months. The Green Movement's leaders, former Prime Minister Mir-Hossein Mousavi [Khameneh], former parliament speaker Mehdi Karroubi, and former president Mohammad Khatami have opposed sanctions, particularly those that hurt only ordinary Iranians. But, while the sponsors of the Congress sanctions bill pay lip service to the bravery of Iranian people and their courage to push the hard-liners, they also hurt them by imposing such sanctions, because the goal is not to help the Iranian people, but satisfy Israel and its lobby.

While the sponsors of the ... sanctions bill pay lip service to the bravery of Iranian people ..., they also hurt them by imposing ... sanctions.

No Need for Sanctions

If the purpose of such legislation is to hurt Iran's economy to the point that it would cripple the hard-liners and prevent them from pursuing their nuclear program, there is no need for them. First of all, Iran's nuclear program has significantly slowed down, due to both the internal crisis and technical difficulty. The Obama administration concedes that, even if Iran were to produce a nuclear weapon, it does not have a breakout capability for up to three years, ample time for both diplomacy and to see where Iran's internal developments take the nation.

Secondly, [Iranian president] Mahmoud Ahmadinejad's economic policy—if it can be called as such—is already damaging Iran's economy and people's economic welfare greatly. Inflation is rampant, to the point that the government is seriously thinking about devaluing Iran's currency, the rial. Beginning in the upcoming Iranian New Year that will start on March 21, Ahmadinejad will eliminate all the subsidies to basic commodities, foodstuff, etc., and will remove all price controls. Iran's most prominent economists have warned that the action will increase the rate of inflation to 60 percent (from its current official rate of close to 30 percent), further impoverish millions of Iranians, and ruin many businesses.

In addition, Iran has a labor movement that is increasingly stronger and more vocal.

The movement is demanding better pay, more labor-friendly laws, uprooting of corruption, and cutting off the hands of the IRGC from the economy. The labor movement only adds strength to the Green Movement.

Therefore, Iran's internal developments and dynamics are doing what even the best-intentioned pieces of legislation by foreign powers cannot achieve, namely, making the Iranian people even more determined to push for a democratic political system, rule of law, and a completely free press that would reveal the depth of corruption and mismanagement by the hard-liners that are the root cause of the terrible economic situation in Iran.

Iranian people do not need, nor have they called for, foreign interference in their internal affairs (which the gasoline legislation intends). They can address their problems by themselves. What they need are moral support and strong and meaningful condemnation of the gross violations of human rights that are daily occurrences in Iran.

If sanctions are to be imposed, they should strip away the power of the hard-liners to block the free flow of information by making available to Iranian people the technology to break the hard-liners' grip on the Internet, blocking Web sites, and slowing down the Internet traffic and other means of mass communication. If sanctions are to be imposed, they should isolate the IRGC leaders and their allies in Iran's conservative camp, not hurting Iranians just when their century-old struggle for democracy is beginning to bear fruit.

A Military Strike Against Iran Is a Feasible and Credible Option

Chuck Wald

Chuck Wald is a retired U.S. Air Force four-star general who was the air commander for the initial stages of Operation Enduring Freedom in Afghanistan and deputy commander of the U.S. European Command.

In a policy address at the Council on Foreign Relations last month [July 2009], Secretary of State Hillary Clinton said of Iran, "We cannot be afraid or unwilling to engage." But the Iranian government has yet to accept President [Barack] Obama's outstretched hand. Even if Tehran [capital of Iran] suddenly acceded to talks, U.S. policy makers must prepare for the eventuality that diplomacy fails. While there has been much discussion of economic sanctions, we cannot neglect the military's role in a Plan B.

The Role of Military Tools

There has been a lack of serious public discussion of the military tools available to us. Any mention of them is either met with accusations of warmongering or hushed with concerns over sharing sensitive information. It is important to discuss, within legal limits, such a serious issue as openly as possible. Discussion strengthens our democracy and dispels misinformation.

The military can play an important role in solving this complex problem without firing a single shot. Publicly signaling serious preparation for a military strike might obviate the need for one if deployments force Tehran to recognize the costs of its nuclear defiance. Mr. Obama might consider, for example, the deployment of additional carrier battle groups and minesweepers to the waters off Iran, and the conduct of military exercises with allies.

After all other diplomatic avenues and economic pressures have been exhausted, the U.S. military is capable of launching a devastating attack on Iranian nuclear and military facilities.

If such pressure fails to impress Iranian leadership, the U.S. Navy could move to blockade Iranian ports. A blockade—which is an act of war—would effectively cut off Iran's gasoline imports, which constitute about one-third of its consumption. Especially in the aftermath of post-election protests, the Iranian leadership must worry about the economic dislocations and political impact of such action.

Should these measures not compel Tehran to reverse course on its nuclear program, and only after all other diplomatic avenues and economic pressures have been exhausted, the U.S. military is capable of launching a devastating attack on Iranian nuclear and military facilities.

A Military Option Is Viable

Many policy makers and journalists dismiss the military option on the basis of a false sense of futility. They assume that the U.S. military is already overstretched, that we lack adequate intelligence about the location of covert nuclear sites, and that known sites are too heavily fortified.

Such assumptions are false.

An attack on Iranian nuclear facilities would mostly involve air assets, primarily Air Force and Navy, that are not strained by operations in Iraq and Afghanistan. Moreover, the presence of U.S. forces in countries that border Iran offers dis-

163

tinct advantages. Special Forces and intelligence personnel already in the region can easily move to protect key assets or perform clandestine operations. It would be prudent to emplace additional missile-defense capabilities in the region, upgrade both regional facilities and allied militaries, and expand strategic partnerships with countries such as Azerbaijan and Georgia to pressure Iran from all directions.

Conflict may reveal previously undetected Iranian facilities as Iranian forces move to protect them. Moreover, nuclear sites buried underground may survive sustained bombing, but their entrances and exits will not.

While a successful bombing campaign would set back Iranian nuclear development, Iran would undoubtedly retain its nuclear know-how.

The Risks of Military Action

Of course, there are huge risks to military action: U.S. and allied casualties; rallying Iranians around an unstable and oppressive regime; Iranian reprisals be they direct or by proxy against us and our allies; and Iranian-instigated unrest in the Persian Gulf states, first and foremost in Iraq.

Furthermore, while a successful bombing campaign would set back Iranian nuclear development, Iran would undoubtedly retain its nuclear know-how. An attack would also necessitate years of continued vigilance, both to retain the ability to strike previously undiscovered sites and to ensure that Iran does not revive its nuclear program.

But the risks of military action must be weighed against those of doing nothing. If the Iranian regime continues to advance its nuclear program despite the best efforts of Mr. Obama and other world leaders, we risk Iranian domination of the oil-rich Persian Gulf, threats to U.S.-allied Arab regimes, the emboldening of radicals in the region, the creation of an existential threat to Israel, the destabilization of Iraq, the shutdown of the Israel-Palestinian peace process, and a regional nuclear arms race.

A peaceful resolution of the threat posed by Iran's nuclear ambitions would certainly be the best possible outcome. But should diplomacy and economic pressure fail, a U.S. military strike against Iran is a technically feasible and credible option.

More Creative, Flexible Negotiations Are Necessary to Reach Agreement with Iran

Center for Strategic & International Studies

The Center for Strategic & International Studies (CSIS) is a bipartisan, nonprofit research organization that provides policy analysis and proposals to policy makers and the public.

Iran continues to steal the headlines: There's increasing momentum for a new round of sanctions to prevent Iran from importing refined gasoline, and the U.S. and European leaders are discussing what to do next.... [U.S. president Barack] Obama set a September [2009] deadline for progress on negotiations. Recently, Iran has said they're willing to negotiate. A CNN article quoted Iran's negotiator saying they are ready to negotiate,

> Saeed Jalili, Iran's top nuclear negotiator, said Iran would open talks and offer new proposals, according to a TV report aired on Tuesday [September 1, 2009]. "The package being offered by the Islamic Republic of Iran is updated and ready to be presented," Jalili said. "We hope [the new] round of talks will be held to help the world feel progress, justice and peace." Jalili did not say what the new package entailed.

However, some are skeptical that Iran will make any meaningful changes in their offer. They argue that Iran has no intention of altering its nuclear program and instead is trying to appear just cooperative enough to block a new round of sanctions. This view isn't unfounded; Iran has, in the past, taken advantage of negotiations to continue developing their nuclear program. Also, the reaction to the recent IAEA [International Atomic Energy Agency] report leaves questions about Iran's intentions,

> "There remain a number of outstanding issues which give rise to concerns and which need to be clarified to exclude the existence of possible military dimensions to Iran's nuclear program," said the text of the IAEA report, as quoted by the Associated Press. It said the IAEA "does not consider that Iran has adequately addressed the substance of the issues, having focused instead on the style and form . . . and providing limited answers and simple denials."

Current Negotiations Are Failing

The problem is that the debate about how to respond goes back and forth between extremes. Some argue that we should impose sanctions and consider strikes without ever participating in negotiations, while others say we should take military threats and sanctions off the table to decrease enmity and convince Iran that they don't need nuclear weapons. What we need is a more nuanced middle ground.

Some argue that we should impose sanctions and consider strikes . . . while others say we should take military threats and sanctions off the table. . . . What we need is a . . . middle ground.

The fundamental problem is less that engagement or sanctions are the wrong approach, and more that neither side has proposed a solution that the other considers acceptable. The U.S. and Israel, so far, have been unwilling to live with Iran having access to the full fuel cycle, while Iran is unwilling to abandon its right to peaceful enrichment. The stalemate was described quite well in a recent *Time* report,

"We can expect that the new Iranian package, much like the most recent Western proposals presented to Iran, will mostly be a repackaging of old positions," says Trita Parsi, an Iran analyst and president of the National Iranian American Council. Until now, Western governments have demanded that Iran suspend its uranium-enrichment program and negotiate an agreement to relinquish it in exchange for a package of economic incentives. But Iran insists that its much-scrutinized enrichment is for peaceful purposes, which it claims as a right under the Nuclear Non-Proliferation Treaty [Treaty on the Non-Proliferation of Nuclear Weapons]. Its proposals to resolve the standoff have typically focused on strengthening international safeguards against the weaponization of its enrichment facilities. Parsi expects that, at best, the Iranian package will suggest ways of strengthening the international inspection regime. "That's very valuable in itself," he says, "but it's short of what the U.S. has been demanding so far."

Thus far, the two sides have offered diametrically opposed solutions to the problem that uranium-enrichment capability can be adapted to develop nuclear weapons material. The West has insisted that because Iran's intentions are under a cloud of suspicion, it must forgo enriching uranium and instead agree to import its reactor fuel. The Iranians, when they've been in an engaging mood, have focused on reinforcing international safeguards against weaponization. But Tehran [capital of Iran] hasn't been in an engaging mood for some time now. It showed little interest in the U.S.-backed European proposal of a "freeze-for-freeze" formula, under which Iran would desist from expanding its enrichment capacity in exchange for Western powers' refraining from adopting new sanctions. Nor has Tehran given more than a desultory response to Obama's offer of talks.

The same article cites critics who believe that the current negotiating posture, of insisting on a suspension of enrichment, will fail,

Some influential voices in the West have questioned the viability of demanding that Tehran give up enrichment altogether. Senate Foreign Relations Committee chairman John Kerry said in June that it was "ridiculous" to make Tehran's surrender of that right a condition for a diplomatic solution. "They have a right to peaceful nuclear power and to enrichment in that purpose," Kerry told the *Financial Times.* But there has been no change in the official U.S. position. Revulsion over the Iranian regime's handling of its June presidential election has further narrowed Obama's room for diplomatic engagement with Iran. And Obama is under growing pressure from key actors like Israel as well as from Capitol Hill and his administration to ratchet up the pressure.

The U.S. and Israel, so far, have been unwilling to live with Iran having access to the full fuel cycle, while Iran is unwilling to abandon its right to peaceful enrichment.

However, it comes short by failing to offer an alternative proposal or negotiating strategy that could be effective.

More Creative Negotiations: An International Fuel Bank?

One idea could be to go back to a proposal that was supported by the Obama administration earlier this year: an international fuel bank. Obama considered the fuel bank to be part of the agenda of "getting to zero",

> The Obama administration is specifically supporting the development of an international nuclear fuel bank that aspiring nuclear-power states could tap to feed their reactors.

> Such a system, say U.S. officials, would undercut demands of countries like North Korea and Iran that they need to develop their own infrastructure to produce nuclear fuel. Such technologies can be easily shifted into producing fissile material for nuclear weapons.

A senior Obama administration official disclosed Sunday that, as part of that effort, the White House has had high-level contact in recent weeks with Kazakhstan to serve as host for such a proposed fuel bank. The White House is seriously considering the offer, and transferring control of the operation to the UN's nuclear watchdog, the International Atomic Energy Agency. Only countries that renounce nuclear weapons and the production of nuclear fuel could take part in the program, said the official.

The IAEA has for years supported the idea of a nuclear fuel bank, and it's been understood that it would help monitor the facility.

The fuel bank is not a new proposal and has, in the past, been opposed, by both nuclear and non-nuclear states,

The idea is not new. The 1946 "Baruch Plan" proposed by the United States sought to establish such a global fuel bank. More recently, the Director General of the IAEA, Mohamed ElBaradei, has endorsed a similar concept. The fuel bank idea is gradually gaining international support but has yet to materialize.

To work, an international fuel bank would have to be a fail-safe, incentive-based consortium under which countries would be 100 percent certain to gain unlimited access to reactor fuel in exchange for forgoing indigenous enrichment and reprocessing facilities and adopting stringent safeguard measures.

The devil is in the details, however, and it is not yet clear who will supply the fuel bank and surrender their national right to determine the end user of its contributed fuel. For their part, non-nuclear-weapon states are understandably reticent to surrender additional rights in a world where nuclear disarmament remains an uncertain prospect.

Thus any attempt at creating an international fuel bank will encounter stiff resistance, as it will essentially call for revisiting the agreements set out in the 1968 Treaty on the Non-Proliferation of Nuclear Weapons. But nuclear-weapon states will have to be prepared to compromise if they wish to enlist support for the initiative.

To be viable, more tangible steps by today's nuclear powers must be made toward verifiable nuclear disarmament, complemented with a new push to implement the stalled Comprehensive [Nuclear-]Test-Ban Treaty and negotiations on an agreement banning further production of fissile material.

One idea could be to go back to a proposal that was supported by the Obama administration earlier this year: an international fuel bank.

However, despite opposition, the fuel bank has promise because there has been preliminary support in the U.S., Russia, and some European countries, but also in Iran. In response to Obama's proposal, Iran seemed interested in the idea,

Iran welcomed on Monday a proposal to set up a global nuclear fuel repository, part of a U.S.-backed plan to put all uranium enrichment under strict international control.

President Mahmoud Ahmadinejad, in Kazakhstan on a visit, said he supported a proposal to host the nuclear bank in the fellow Caspian nation, which is accessible from Iran by sea.

"We think that (Kazakh President) Nursultan Nazarbayev's idea to host a nuclear fuel bank is a very good proposal," he told reporters after talks with the Kazakh leader.

Iran's support for the idea comes as U.S. President Barack Obama pushes for a "new beginning" in bilateral ties, and could play a role in mending bridges after decades of mistrust.

Iran has said before that it would consider stopping sensitive uranium enrichment if guaranteed a supply of nuclear fuel from abroad. However, it has also frequently insisted on its right to master the complete nuclear fuel cycle, including enriching uranium, for peaceful purposes.

There was also support from [Ali] Larijani,

The former secretary of Iran's Supreme National Security Council Ali Larijani announced, "We back the idea of establishing an international nuclear fuel bank."

Theoretical Benefits of a Fuel Bank

While some version of a fuel bank has been proposed on numerous occasions, the details have never been worked out. In recent proposals, the fuel bank would be hosted in either Russia or Kazakhstan, be run by the IAEA, and sell nuclear fuel to any countries that wanted it.

Nonproliferation advocates see a lot of promise in the fuel bank. They argue that the spread of nuclear power makes it too easy for [a] country to convert peaceful nuclear power programs to nuclear weapons programs. A fuel bank would solve this concern because countries would not need to develop their own nuclear program to have access to nuclear energy. Therefore, the fuel bank could be a "litmus test" for proliferation. If a country wanted to develop a nuclear power program, and claimed they were doing so because of energy needs, their motivations would be suspect if a stable supply of nuclear fuel was available from a fuel bank. Joe Cirincione, an advocate of the fuel bank, who sees it as a potential solution to the deadlock with Iran, describes its benefits,

First, it has the potential to address Iran's concerns about security of fuel supply. An international fuel bank that is country-neutral, durable, and governed by objective criteria is more likely to attract Iranian support than a *sui generis* [Latin for "its own kind"] mechanism created specifically to deal with Iran. Second, a fuel bank push would head off the regional proliferation consequences of Iran suddenly announcing its nuclear- or near-nuclear capability. At the very least, the existence of a credible nuclear fuel bank would make it harder for Iran's Sunni Arab neighbors to pursue any nuclear weapons ambitions under the guise of nuclear energy development. Third, a nuclear fuel bank could serve as a first step towards more ambitious, global efforts to prevent the abuse of nuclear-fuel-cycle technology. That's why the United States should press ahead with the fuel bank proposal with or without Iran's support. This initiative would reduce the chances of a "virtual" arms race in the region by controlling the most sensitive component of the nuclear fuel cycle, uranium enrichment. The possibility that Iran may be left out of such an important initiative may also serve as an added inducement for Iran to forego uranium enrichment.

It is clear from his description that Cirincione is proposing a fuel bank that is located outside of Iran's soil, but Iran would have access to. While this solution would provide a high level of confidence for Europe, the U.S., and Israel, it might not be acceptable to Iran. . . .

If a country wanted to develop a nuclear power program . . . [for] energy needs, their motivations would be suspect if a stable supply of nuclear fuel was available from a fuel bank.

It's Good for Iran . . . but Why Should the United States Do It?

The main benefit of this proposal is that it provides a real opportunity to find a negotiated solution. Iran has demonstrated that they are not willing to back down on the enrichment issue. A new round of sanctions is unlikely to change that. Unless we find a middle ground, the U.S. will be forced to accept an Iranian nuclear capability or start another military conflict in the Middle East.

However, a fuel bank or internationally monitored facility is not just a way to avoid war, it also solves current concerns with Iran's nuclear program. First, it could be sold as a political victory. Obama could say that he has found a way to ensure that Iran has no nuclear weapons program, while advancing the world toward global zero. An international consortium is the one solution that allows both Iranian and U.S. leaders to declare victory, and is therefore the most likely to be accepted by both sides. Second, this proposal would ease proliferation concerns. The facility, while on Iranian soil, would be run in cooperation with the international community. Current IAEA challenge inspections are seen as ineffective because they give Iran too much of an opportunity to divert nuclear fuel to a weapons program, but a permanent IAEA presence would alleviate those concerns. Dr. Geoffrey Forden and Sir John Thomson, who advocate this proposal and have written about it a few times, believe verification, would be extremely effective,

> The IAEA would be consulted on the design of the plant and would operate three forms of safeguards: full-scope, additional protocol, and specially agreed transparency measures. Each shift of workers would have a majority of non-Iranians and non-Iranians would hold key positions in the management company. Together, these measures would protect both against diversion of material and against the establishment of a clandestine facility. Other security measures, especially "black boxing" and disabling mechanisms are considered.

> The risks of an Iranian "breakout" by expropriating the multilaterally owned facility are minor and the risks that the Iranians would and could establish a clandestine facility are, in comparison with other schemes, negligible.

If Iran tried to kick the IAEA out or build up any other nuclear facility in the country, it would be a clear indication that Iran was seeking to acquire nuclear weapons, allowing the U.S. to respond in kind. Also, just the offer would be a test of

Iranian intentions. If Iran said no to a pilot enrichment facility on their soil that would guarantee access to nuclear fuel, the U.S. and the international community could be fairly certain that Iran intended to acquire nuclear weapons.

The United States Must Increase Support for Iran's Green Movement

Iran Policy Committee

The Iran Policy Committee is a pressure group meant to influence U.S. government policy toward Iran.

During the second half of December 2009, anti-regime protest in Iran accelerated. The latest and most brutally repressed demonstrations centered on the Shiite [one of Iraq's two Muslim sects] holiday of Ashura commemorating the death of Hussein, the most holy Shiite martyr. Regime security forces reportedly fired into crowds of protestors, killing at least ten, wounding hundreds, and arresting hundreds more.

Backing Iran's Green Movement

According to Iran Policy Committee (IPC) President and former member of the National Security Council staff at the White House, Professor Raymond Tanter, "Watching videos of workers and students wearing green ribbons chanting, 'Marg bar dictator!'—'Death to the dictator,' reminds me of youths and workers wearing orange-colored clothing in Ukraine chanting, 'Razom nas bahato! Nas ne podolaty!'—'Together, we are many! We cannot be defeated!' Just as the opposition joined forces together in an 'orange revolution' to prevent the ruling elite from falsifying an election and hijacking Ukraine's presidency, a 'green revolution' in Iran has now gone beyond elections and will bring down the politically corrupt regime in Tehran [capital of Iran]."

Prof. Tanter continued, "As the scale of protest and level of repression have followed an upward trajectory, so has the

Iran Policy Committee, "The Green Iranian Revolution and the American Response," Earthtimes.org, December 29, 2009. Reproduced by permission.

firmness of President [Barack] Obama's response. At the beginning of the June 2009 demonstrations, the Obama administration took a decidedly mild tone in condemning the Iranian regime's use of violence against peaceful protestors. As rationale for such a tone, administration officials cited the imperative of keeping open the door for a negotiated solution to Iran's nuclear program and fear that association with the United States could detract from the protest movement. Faced with such criticism, Obama escalated his rhetoric on 23 June, saying, 'The United States and the international community have been appalled and outraged by the threats, the beatings and imprisonments of the last few days. I strongly condemn these unjust actions.'"

Prof. Tanter stated, "As the prospects of a negotiated settlement on Iran's nuclear program have become all but moot, the Obama administration has become more outspoken in its condemnation of the Iranian regime during the most recent spasm of violence in Iran. National Security Council spokesman Mike Hammer said of the Ashura violence, 'Hope and history are on the side of those who peacefully seek their universal rights, . . . placing the United States firmly on the side of the demonstrators and in opposition to the Iranian regime. This statement mirrors President Obama's Nobel Prize speech in which he ad-libbed regarding the Iranian protestors, 'these movements of hope and history—they have us on their side.'"

As the scale of protest and level of repression [in Iran] have followed an upward trajectory, so has the firmness of President Obama's response.

General Thomas McInerney (Lt. Gen., US Air Force Ret., chair of the IPC Advisory Council), states, "Amid rumors of military defections to the side of the demonstrators, the Iranian regime is as divided as it has been since the days of the 1979 [Iranian] Revolution. During June 2009 protests, several

Islamic Revolutionary Guard Corps commanders were arrested because they refused to get involved in the repression. One leading commander was arrested for arranging a secret meeting with other officers." According to Gen. McInerney, "The most remarkable development in the 'green movement' is the shift in focus from President [Mahmoud] Ahmadinejad as the object of scorn to Ayatollah [Ali] Khamenei, the Supreme Leader. To chant 'Death to Khamenei!' who claims to be God's representative on Earth, highlights the degree to which the entire political system of the Islamic republic has lost its legitimacy in the eyes of its people."

President Obama must increase pressure on the Iranian regime over its appalling human rights record, send a strong signal of support to the Iranian people, and exploit divisions already appearing among the ruling elite.

Stronger Rhetoric Needed

According to MG [Major General] Paul Vallely (US Army Ret., IPC Advisory Council), "With the lights moving to red for engagement and green for regime change, President Obama must increase pressure on the Iranian regime over its appalling human rights record, send a strong signal of support to the Iranian people, and exploit divisions already appearing among the ruling elite."

Gen. Vallely said, "Washington must take note of Tehran's use of propaganda to try and discredit Iran's main dissident group, the Mujahedin-e Khalq (MEK). Iranian official media blamed the MEK for hijacking Ashura festivities to incite violence, which suggests this group is a major player in heightening opposition to the clerical regime. Because the regime pays so much attention to the MEK, the United States must engage Iran's main opposition group by removing it from the U.S.

Foreign Terrorist Organizations list following the lead of the European Union and UK [United Kingdom], both of which delisted the MEK."

According to R. Bruce McColm (President of the Institute for Democratic Strategies, IPC Board of Directors), "An important distinction to make is between Iran's loyal and disloyal opposition. Initially, protests revolved around support for Ahmadinejad's main electoral rival, Mir-Hossein Mousavi [Khameneh], who is part of Iran's 'loyal opposition,' in the sense that he in no way opposed the legitimacy of the clerical regime. As the regime used more violence, though, activists became less enamored of Mousavi and began protesting against the entire system, not only the fraudulent election, and became a 'disloyal opposition' movement. Some went as far as to burn photos of not only the Supreme Leader, Ayatollah Khamenei, but also the founder of the Islamic republic, Ayatollah [Ruhollah] Khomeini, thus breaking an untouchable taboo. Such disloyal actions brought the spontaneous street protesters more in line with opposition groups, such as the MEK, which had long questioned the legitimacy of the Islamic republic."

According to IPC President and former member of the National Security Council staff at the White House, Professor Raymond Tanter, "While State repression helps unify the opposition, the clerical elites are developing fissures as their legitimacy is called into question. 'Crippling sanctions' would exacerbate such splits and increase the likelihood that the cycle of peaceful protest and State violence leads to the kind of regime change that vastly reduces the threat of Iran's nuclear program. Meanwhile, stronger rhetoric from President Obama should highlight the egregious human rights violations of the Iranian regime, nobility of those Iranians who sacrifice their bodies to protest for democracy, and commitment of the United States to the principle of self-determination for all peoples. In this respect, President Obama would give the 'green revolution,' which is no longer led by former presidential candidates, the push it needs to change the regime in Tehran."

The United States Should Recognize Iran as a Peaceful Nuclear Power

Kayhan Barzegar

Kayhan Barzegar is an assistant professor of international relations at Science and Research Campus, Islamic Azad University; a senior research fellow at the Center for Middle East Strategic Studies in Tehran; and a research fellow at the Belfer Center for Science and International Affairs at Harvard University.

During President Mahmoud Ahmadinejad's first term, Iranian foreign policy had two key enduring components. First, Tehran [Iran's capital] sought to deal with Iran's new security dilemma brought about by the U.S. presence in both Iraq and Afghanistan after 2003. Iran responded with an "accommodating policy," which consisted of expanding cooperation after Saddam's [referring to former Iraqi leader Saddam Hussein] fall with the main Arab world actors, principally Egypt and Saudi Arabia, and seeking direct talks with the United States. This included Iran's engagement in direct talks with Coalition Forces regarding the prevailing security situations in both Iraq and Afghanistan. In this way, Iran hoped to avoid both a new round of rivalry with its Arab neighbors and a new security dilemma in its relations with the United States.

The second component was to seek an "alliance policy" while regionalizing the nuclear issue, in which Iran sought to tie and interweave the nuclear issue with broader regional dynamics such as Israel's undeclared nuclear arsenal and the Arab-Israeli conflict. By building relationships with friendly

Kayhan Barzegar, "Iran's Foreign Policy Strategy After Saddam," *The Washington Quarterly*, vol. 33, January 10, 2010, pp. 173–174, 179–181, 183–187. Copyright © 2010 Center for Strategic and International Studies. Reproduced by permission of the Publisher and the author.

states (e.g., Syria) and political movements (e.g., Hezbollah [a group in Lebanon] or Shi'ite factions in Iraq), Iran tried to deter the U.S. or Israeli military threat in the short term and to prevent the institutionalization of a U.S. role in its backyard in the long term.

The prevailing view in the United States is that Ahmadinejad's foreign policy and Iran's increasing presence in the region has been offensive, expansionist, opportunistic, and often ideological. Though Iran has occasionally taken advantage of new opportunities, these characterizations have been exaggerated in the United States. Instead, Iran's action should be perceived in a more pragmatic light. Though Ahmadinejad may himself be an ideological and divisive figure, Iran's foreign policy strategy predates him and ought to be viewed as a wider Iranian effort to secure its geostrategic interests and national security concerns. Despite Ahmadinejad's tendencies to indulge his eccentricities, the logic of Iran's foreign policy decision-making process always ensures this return to pragmatism.

If the Iranian leadership's actions are perceived as offensive and expansionist, then the rational choice for the United States is to maintain robust *deterrence*. In contrast, if Iran's policies are defensive, then the rational choice for the United States is to seek *cooperation* with Iran and eventually to help integrate Iran into the regional political-security architecture. Such integration is certainly inseparable from settling the ongoing nuclear dispute and reaching a broader and much anticipated détente with the United States. It is essential that Washington not misinterpret Iran's actions. Misreading Iran prevented the [George W.] Bush administration from pursuing engagement and cooperation. President Barack Obama must not make the same mistake. He should reexamine the current perception of Iran's regional aims and redefine Iran's place in U.S. Middle East policy.

After Iran's June 2009 presidential election, Western commentators and policy makers have speculated about divisions among the Iranian political elite, and how to exploit them to gain leverage on Iran's nuclear program and various outstanding regional disputes. Such a policy, however, will bear little fruit. Though there are of course differences of style and approach among the elite, it is clear that Iran's nuclear program has the capability to unite them, especially in the face of foreign threats of increased sanctions and military attack. What, therefore, should be the Obama administration's stance toward Ahmadinejad's second term in office?. . .

If Iran's policies are defensive, then the rational choice for the United States is to seek cooperation with Iran.

Iran's Foreign Policy and Defense Strategy

Iran currently views security in the region as a non-zero-sum game in which the best action for securing Iran's national interests is to advance a win-win game. Iran knows that the United States has vital interests in Iraq, as well as the region at large, and is not likely to leave the region completely. Iran also knows that the public, in both the United States and the region, will not welcome a long-term U.S. presence. From Iran's perspective, therefore, a feasible middle ground is to help the United States secure its interests without an excessive regional presence. The strategic value of this deal is to establish a new kind of balance of interests and balance of security between Iran and the United States. In this respect, Iran's previous cooperation with the United States and other regional actors in settling the Afghanistan crisis in 2001 is a vivid example.

Likewise, advancing cooperation with the United States and other relevant regional actors in settling Iraq's insecurity is another sign of Iran's pragmatic inclinations. The strong willingness to proceed with direct talks with the United States on Iraq's security issues means that Iran has strategically accepted the role of the United States in Iraq. Tehran simply seeks to minimize the threat posed by the U.S. presence in the region through cooperation and engagement. In this manner, Iran has decided to advance a win-win game. Similarly, Iran has been very cautious not to engage directly in any conflict with the United States in Iraq and the Persian Gulf. Regarding the relations with other major actors in the region, such as Saudi Arabia and Egypt, Iran has pursued a strategy of maintaining amicable relationships mostly through reassurance and cooperation. For instance, Iran has attempted to advance regional cooperation by actively participating in regional conferences regarding the crises in Iraq and Lebanon.

[Iran] simply seeks to minimize the threat posed by the U.S. presence in the region through cooperation and engagement.

Yet, from a strategic point of view, Iran's geopolitical position, its sources of power, and unique political-cultural dynamics require that it take on a greater regional presence than it has in the past. Tehran's political elite views Iran's increased regional involvement as imperative, notwithstanding the numerous cosmetic changes that have accompanied the Obama administration's "reorientation" about Iran. This rationale is based on three fundamentally defensive policy assumptions:

An Insecure and Unstable Neighborhood. Living in an unstable neighborhood has been costly for Iran over the past decades. The continued instability and sectarian conflict across the western border (Iraq), failed and unstable states in the east (Afghanistan and Pakistan), transforming states in the north (Central Asia and the Caucasus), and authoritarian and security dependent regimes in the south and Persian Gulf, each subject to political-social changes in the future, have formed the basis for Iran's insecure and unstable backyard. Such an insecure environment has the potential to spread regional rivalries, military conflict, crises, and subsequently foreign powers' presence. The revival of the Taliban in Afghanistan in recent years is a pertinent example. A major portion of Iran's political and economic stamina is being spent on tackling these varied threats in the region. The need to continuously maintain a powerful army to protect Iran's national borders is rooted in this dimension of Iran's national security demands. The Shah's regime [referring to Iran's former King Mohammad Reza Shah Pahlavi], for instance, justified the perpetuation of a great Iranian army to tackle future military threats from the Iraqi Ba'athist regime [Iraq's government under Saddam Hussein].

Interconnected Security. To tackle the threats emerging on its immediate borders, Iran's defense strategy has mainly focused on constructing the concept of "interconnected security," which means having an "offensive defense" or defense through active military engagement. From the perspective of Iranian governing elites, the region's security has been seen as synonymous with Iran's security and vice versa. Iran is paying a great price for preserving regional security, without receiving appropriate gains in return. If the region's security is significant to the United States and regional states, there needs to be an acknowledgement of the reality that Iran is an essential part of the region's security system. Iran will not continue to ensure that the region is secure at the expense of Iran's own insecurity. . . .

Preempting Future Security Threats. Iran's geopolitical realities, ethnic politics, and cultural-religious characteristics intimately tie its national security to that of the region as a whole. To preempt future security threats, Iran reserves the right to modestly engage in the region's political and economic architecture and activities. With the acquisition of a greater role, effective responsibility, and assurances that it can preempt future threats, Iran will be able to use its political and military energy for the sake of economic and political development. Viewed in this context, establishing bilateral and mutual economic, cultural, and political-security agreements with neighboring states will lead the region toward greater stability and mutual cooperation. Iran's engagement in Iraq is aimed at preempting future challenges. By supporting those political factions or groups in Iraq that are, in a remarkable break with the past, friendlier today toward Iran and unwilling to participate in an anti-Iranian coalition for the foreseeable future, Tehran has attempted to coax Baghdad [capital of Iraq] into fulfilling the role of a strategic partner in the region. . . .

The Comprehensive Package Deal

Negotiating on several disparate fronts is not in Iran's or the region's interests, nor will it lead to a lasting settlement. The single most effective route is to accept the aforesaid mutual areas of concern as a comprehensive package, which would afford Iran strategic parity in the course of negotiations. Only then will Iran feel confident enough to make genuine concessions and acquire the assurances it has long sought. Iran's security strategy in this context is more defensive and based on an interconnected security and concomitant domino effect: Iran's security is equivalent to regional security, and Iran's insecurity will produce regional insecurity. Building alliances and coalitions with friendly factions in Iraq, Syria, and Lebanon are thus aimed to support Iran's reactionary defensive foreign policy, supporting the fact that Iran's decisive engagement in the region is pragmatic in nature. Three issues will now dominate Iran's foreign policy: the nuclear issue, U.S.-Iran bilateral relations, and outstanding regional disputes.

The Iranian leadership knows very well that only the nuclear issue has the power to bring the United States to the negotiating table and provide impetus for a settlement of other outstanding issues of "secondary" concern. The nuclear program serves as a point of convergence in which U.S.-Iran interests coincide and thereby has the unrivalled potential to act as a catalyst to reconcile any outstanding issues and grievances. Unlike other issues of foreign policy over which there may be disagreement or vigorous debate, when it comes to the nuclear issue and Iran's preservation of its independent nuclear fuel cycle, there is a strong elite consensus that runs across the political spectrum. Moreover, despite recent post-election controversies, the nuclear issue continues to have domestic grassroots support, and the continued potential to act as a source of legitimacy for the Ahmadinejad government in the face of foreign criticism. Today, the nuclear program is perceived as a matter of technological advancement, national pride, and solidarity that bolsters Iranian identity and status regionally and internationally. Consequently, all political parties in Iran demand the pursuit of a tough stance in talks on the nuclear program. The nuclear program, therefore, is beyond standard reformist or hard-line policy disagreements—there is only one line and that is the line of national interest.

Among elite support, the program has the backing of supreme leader [Ali] Khamenei. Iran's numerous legislative, judicial, executive, and military bodies, along with the supreme leader, have representatives at the National Security Council, which is the main body that decides the direction of Iran's foreign policy. Despite differences that exist among all bodies and representatives, the council ensures a consensus among them. Hence, Western efforts to try to exploit apparent elite divisions in Iran—which have largely subsided in the months following the presidential election—will not be successful. Furthermore, Ahmadinejad will continue to pursue his proactive foreign policy to counter Western pressure, if Washington refuses to take genuine steps toward a substantive change in policy. The United States needs to formulate a long-term strategic perspective instead of making short-lived and fleeting gains due to a miscalculated and erroneous understanding of the significance and future of Iranian politics after its presidential election.

At present, the main controversy between Iran and the United States is who should take the first step, and what that step should be. While the Bush administration spoke of preconditions and demanded suspending uranium enrichment, the Obama administration has spoken of negotiations without preconditions but arguably has fallen into old patterns by setting vague and unilateral deadlines in late September 2009. Diplomacy is undoubtedly a painstaking and time-consuming process, but Iran has agreed to open its Qom facility to International Atomic Energy Agency inspectors. Very quickly in the course of the October 2009 Geneva talks, Tehran has further agreed to send its declared enriched uranium to Russia for processing. Though Obama's reaction to the Iranian presidential election was measured, the belief that Washington can exploit apparent divisions within Iran's elite is gaining ground, as witnessed by many of the sentiments expressed in the House Foreign Affairs Committee hearings on Iran in July 2009, which tried to make sense of Iran's post-election developments.

The Iranian leadership knows very well that only the nuclear issue has the power to bring the United States to the negotiating table.

Such a strategy, however, will fail for several reasons. First, Ahmadinejad has the confidence and support of Khamenei, who has final authorization over policy. In fact, it would have been nearly impossible for a strong reformist candidate to proceed in forging ahead with a U.S.-Iran détente—the deeply entrenched institutional obstacles to such action would have made such a feat nearly impossible. Ahmadinejad, however, is eager to forge ahead along the path of U.S.-Iran diplomacy. The question, of course, is whether the Obama administration will continue along the diplomatic trajectory outlined by Obama in the U.S. presidential campaign and following his inauguration, or whether the administration will return to delusions of regime change in the hopes of destabilizing Iran and extracting gains from the Iranian leadership, which will prove unacceptable to all across the Iranian political spectrum.

Furthermore, regional issues cannot be isolated from the broader picture. By initiating an active foreign policy and engaging decisively in places such as Afghanistan, Gaza, Iraq, and Lebanon, Iran has been comparable to the United States, providing Iran with the opportunity to reorient the region's traditional zero-sum game to a win-win game. Regional activeness has offered Iran the opportunity to redefine its role in its security backyard, especially in the Persian Gulf and Iraq. In fact, Iran's active presence in the three rounds of direct talks with the United States on Iraq's political-security issues was the result of Iran's increased regional role.

Iran's nuclear program has certainly presented the option of direct talks. Now, the desire to hold direct talks is present on both the U.S. and Iranian sides. In Washington, Iran's increased role in the region, as well as its involvement in important global and strategic issues, has made engagement inevitable. In Tehran, having a strong and comparable stance vis-à-vis the United States on regional issues, together with Iran's self-reliance in tackling perceived U.S. military threats, has intensified internal desires to start direct talks.

If Obama, however, falls into the trap of resorting to the threats and dogmatic policies adopted by his predecessors, a historic opportunity could well be missed. Iraq and Afghanistan are far from stabilized and Iran could prove vital to bring lasting security to the region. Ahmadinejad, however, will not concede Iran's claim to the nuclear fuel cycle. He has staked far too much of his government's legitimacy and personal credibility on the matter. In any case, the nuclear portfolio has never been under his undisputed control. The important question, as far as the United States is concerned, is whether the

Obama administration is willing to take the courageous step of engaging in meaningful diplomacy, while resisting the temptation to bow to internal and external pressures. Continued attempts to isolate and weaken Iran will only be to the detriment of U.S. goals, which are oriented toward assuring stability, nonproliferation, and the peaceful resolution of ongoing regional conflicts.

The key to solving the Iranian puzzle . . . lies in coming to a realistic and lasting resolution of the nuclear crisis.

The Endgame: What Happens Now?

Policy makers should, therefore, pay close attention to the three key issues which will define Ahmadinejad's second term and the future of U.S.-Iran relations as well as Middle East stability: Iran's defensive foreign policy, the nuclear crisis, and U.S.-Iran détente.

There is no doubt that the key to solving the Iranian puzzle and ameliorating the profound distrust between Iran and the United States lies is coming to a realistic and lasting resolution of the nuclear crisis. It is crucial because it will not only serve as the door to a potential "grand bargain," but may also serve as a vehicle to resolve regional points of contention by facilitating U.S.-Iran cooperation. From Iran's perspective, in the long term, anything less than the continued presence of the independent nuclear fuel cycle on Iranian territory is unacceptable and contrary to the broad and deep-rooted consensus of Iran's political elite. The United States' recognition of Iran as a peaceful nuclear power, in exchange for an international monitoring consortium with U.S. participation based at Iran's nuclear facilities, with rigorous and persuasive guarantees of non-militarization and nonproliferation, might be the only feasible option.

The settlement of the Iranian nuclear crisis should not be seen as separate from the various regional crises, such as Iraq and Afghanistan, and the ongoing tensions and disputes surrounding the Arab-Israeli conflict. Settling the nuclear issue, acknowledging Iran's status as a regional power, and incorporating it into the region's security architecture would allow Iran to work in coordination with the United States, as opposed to playing the roles of strategic adversaries, to bring greater security to the region. If the crisis is resolved and the U.S. military presence is wound down to a level at which Iran's security fears are attenuated—due to the essentially defensive character of Iranian foreign policy—Iranian and U.S. regional aims and goals could move toward coexistence instead of mutual exclusivity.

Ahmadinejad's second term will continue to be proactive, although with greater emphasis on obtaining tangible benefits. The crux of the matter is how the United States will react. If the Obama administration seeks to bring further pressure to bear on Iran in the form of another round of sanctions at the UN [United Nations] Security Council, Obama's promise of reorienting U.S. strategic relations with Iran will be irreparably damaged, and the Iranian leadership's pronouncements of distrust and fears of U.S. doublespeak will be vindicated. Eloquence and pleasant New Year greetings will prove to be far from enough, if there is any hope of breaking the deadlock. Obama has to make a choice between going for long-term stability in a region that is strategically important to the United States and the world or for short-term gains in the futile hope that such leverage will yield a win-lose outcome in which the United States will be the sole victor. The coming weeks will tell the tale.

The United States Must Redefine the Iran Problem

George Friedman

George Friedman is an American political scientist and author. He is the founder, chief intelligence officer, financial overseer, and CEO of the private intelligence corporation STRATFOR.

The United States apparently has reached the point where it must either accept that Iran will develop nuclear weapons at some point if it wishes, or take military action to prevent this. There is a third strategy, however: Washington can seek to redefine the Iranian question.

As we have no idea what leaders on either side are thinking, exploring this represents an exercise in geopolitical theory. Let's begin with the two apparent stark choices.

Diplomacy vs. the Military Option

The diplomatic approach consists of creating a broad coalition prepared to impose what have been called crippling sanctions on Iran. Effective sanctions must be so painful that they compel the target to change its behavior. In Tehran's [referring to Iran's capital] case, this could only consist of blocking Iran's imports of gasoline. Iran imports 35 percent of the gasoline it consumes. It is not clear that a gasoline embargo would be crippling, but it is the only embargo that might work. All other forms of sanctions against Iran would be mere gestures designed to give the impression that something is being done.

The Chinese will not participate in any gasoline embargo. Beijing gets 11 percent of its oil from Iran, and it has made it clear it will continue to deliver gasoline to Iran. Moscow's position is that Russia might consider sanctions down the road,

George Friedman, "The Unthinkable U.S.-Iran Deal," STRATFOR, March 2, 2010. Copyright © 2010. All rights reserved. Reproduced by permission.

but it hasn't specified when, and it hasn't specified what. The Russians are more than content seeing the U.S. bogged down in the Middle East and so are not inclined to solve American problems in the region. With the Chinese and Russians unlikely to embargo gasoline, these sanctions won't create significant pain for Iran. Since all other sanctions are gestures, the diplomatic approach is therefore unlikely to work.

The diplomatic approach is . . . unlikely to work [in Iran].

The military option has its own risks. First, its success depends on the quality of intelligence on Iran's nuclear facilities and on the degree of hardening of those targets. Second, it requires successful air attacks. Third, it requires battle damage assessments that tell the attacker whether the strike succeeded. Fourth, it requires follow-on raids to destroy facilities that remain functional. And fifth, attacks must do more than simply set back Iran's program a few months or even years: If the risk of a nuclear Iran is great enough to justify the risks of war, the outcome must be decisive.

Each point in this process is a potential failure point. Given the multiplicity of these points—which includes others not mentioned—failure may not be an option, but it is certainly possible.

But even if the attacks succeed, the question of what would happen the day after the attacks remains. Iran has its own counters. It has a superbly effective terrorist organization, Hezbollah, at its disposal. It has sufficient influence in Iraq to destabilize that country and force the United States to keep forces in Iraq badly needed elsewhere. And it has the ability to use mines and missiles to attempt to close the Strait of Hormuz and the Persian Gulf shipping lanes for some period— driving global oil prices through the roof while the global economy is struggling to stabilize itself. Iran's position on its nuclear program is rooted in the awareness that while it might not have assured options in the event of a military strike, it has counters that create complex and unacceptable risks. Iran therefore does not believe the United States will strike or permit Israel to strike, as the consequences would be unacceptable.

To recap, the Unites States either can accept a nuclear Iran or risk an attack that might fail outright, impose only a minor delay on Iran's nuclear program or trigger extremely painful responses even if it succeeds. When neither choice is acceptable, it is necessary to find a third choice.

The United States either can accept a nuclear Iran or risk an attack that might fail outfight [or] . . . impose only a minor delay on Iran's nuclear program.

Redefining the Iranian Problem

As long as the problem of Iran is defined in terms of its nuclear program, the United States is in an impossible place. Therefore, the Iranian problem must be redefined. One attempt at redefinition involves hope for an uprising against the current regime. We will not repeat our views on this in depth, but in short, we do not regard these demonstrations to be a serious threat to the regime. Tehran has handily crushed them, and even if they did succeed, we do not believe they would produce a regime any more accommodating toward the United States. The idea of waiting for a revolution is more useful as a justification for inaction—and accepting a nuclear Iran—than it is as a strategic alternative.

At this moment, Iran is the most powerful regional military force in the Persian Gulf. Unless the United States permanently stations substantial military forces in the region, there is no military force able to block Iran. Turkey is more powerful than Iran, but it is far from the Persian Gulf and focused on other matters at the moment, and it doesn't want to take on Iran militarily—at least not for a very long time. At the very least, this means the United States cannot withdraw from Iraq. Baghdad [capital of Iraq] is too weak to block Iran from the Arabian Peninsula, and the Iraqi government has elements friendly toward Iran.

The idea of waiting for a revolution is more useful as a justification for inaction—and accepting a nuclear Iran— than it is as a strategic alternative.

Historically, regional stability depended on the Iraqi-Iranian balance of power. When it tottered in 1990, the result was the Iraqi invasion of Kuwait. The United States did not push into Iraq in 1991 because it did not want to upset the regional balance of power by creating a vacuum in Iraq. Rather, U.S. strategy was to re-establish the Iranian-Iraqi balance of power to the greatest extent possible, as the alternative was basing large numbers of U.S. troops in the region.

The decision to invade Iraq in 2003 assumed that once the Baathist regime [referring to the leadership of Saddam Hussein] was destroyed the United States would rapidly create a strong Iraqi government that would balance Iran. The core mistake in this thinking lay in failing to recognize that the new Iraqi government would be filled with Shiites, many of whom regarded Iran as a friendly power. Rather than balancing Iran, Iraq could well become an Iranian satellite. The Iranians strongly encouraged the American invasion precisely because they wanted to create a situation where Iraq moved toward Iran's orbit. When this in fact began happening, the Americans had no choice but an extended occupation of Iraq, a trap both the [George W.] Bush and [Barack] Obama administrations have sought to escape.

It is difficult to define Iran's influence in Iraq at this point. But at a minimum, while Iran may not be able to impose a pro-Iranian state on Iraq, it has sufficient influence to block the creation of any strong Iraqi government either through direct influence in the government or by creating destabilizing violence in Iraq. In other words, Iran can prevent Iraq from emerging as a counterweight to Iran, and Iran has every reason to do this. Indeed, it is doing just this.

The Fundamental U.S.-Iranian Issue

Iraq, not nuclear weapons, is the fundamental issue between Iran and the United States. Iran wants to see a U.S. withdrawal from Iraq so Iran can assume its place as the dominant military power in the Persian Gulf. The United States wants to withdraw from Iraq because it faces challenges in Afghanistan—where it will also need Iranian cooperation—and elsewhere. Committing forces to Iraq for an extended period of time while fighting in Afghanistan leaves the United States exposed globally. Events involving China or Russia—such as the 2008 war in Georgia—would see the United States without a counter. The alternative would be a withdrawal from Afghanistan or a massive increase in U.S. armed forces. The former is not going to happen any time soon, and the latter is an economic impossibility.

Iraq, not nuclear weapons, is the fundamental issue between Iran and the United States.

Therefore, the United States must find a way to counterbalance Iran without an open-ended deployment in Iraq and without expecting the re-emergence of Iraqi power, because Iran is not going to allow the latter to happen. The nuclear issue is simply an element of this broader geopolitical problem, as it adds another element to the Iranian tool kit. It is not a stand-alone issue.

The United States has an interesting strategy in redefining problems that involves creating extraordinary alliances with mortal ideological and geopolitical enemies to achieve strategic U.S. goals. First consider Franklin Roosevelt's alliance with Stalinist [referring to Russian leader Joseph Stalin] Russia to block Nazi Germany. He pursued this alliance despite massive political outrage not only from isolationists but also from institutions like the Roman Catholic Church that regarded the Soviets as the epitome of evil.

Now consider Richard Nixon's decision to align with China at a time when the Chinese were supplying weapons to North Vietnam that were killing American troops. Moreover, Mao [Zedong]—who had said he did not fear nuclear war as China could absorb a few hundred million deaths—was considered, with reason, quite mad. Nevertheless, Nixon, as anti-Communist and anti-Chinese a figure as existed in American politics, understood that an alliance (and despite the lack of a formal treaty, alliance it was) with China was essential to counterbalance the Soviet Union at a time when American power was still being sapped in Vietnam.

Roosevelt and Nixon both faced impossible strategic situations unless they were prepared to redefine the strategic equation dramatically and accept the need for alliance with countries that had previously been regarded as strategic and moral threats. American history is filled with opportunistic alliances designed to solve impossible strategic dilemmas. The Stalin and Mao cases represent stunning alliances with prior enemies designed to block a third power seen as more dangerous.

It is said that [Iranian president Mahmoud] Ahmadinejad is crazy. It was also said that Mao and Stalin were crazy, in both cases with much justification. Ahmadinejad has said many strange things and issued numerous threats. But when Roosevelt ignored what Stalin said and Nixon ignored what Mao said, they each discovered that Stalin's and Mao's actions were far more rational and predictable than their rhetoric. Similarly, what the Iranians say and what they do are quite different.

U.S. vs. Iranian Interests

Consider the American interest. First, it must maintain the flow of oil through the Strait of Hormuz. The United States cannot tolerate interruptions, and that limits the risks it can take. Second, it must try to keep any one power from controlling all of the oil in the Persian Gulf, as that would give such a country too much long-term power within the global system. Third, while the United States is involved in a war with elements of the Sunni Muslim world, it must reduce the forces devoted to that war. Fourth, it must deal with the Iranian problem directly. Europe will go as far as sanction but no further, while the Russians and Chinese won't even go that far yet. Fifth, it must prevent an Israeli strike on Iran for the same reasons it must avoid a strike itself, as the day after any Israeli strike will be left to the United States to manage.

Now consider the Iranian interest. First, it must guarantee regime survival. It sees the United States as dangerous and unpredictable. In less than 10 years, it has found itself with American troops on both its eastern and western borders. Second, it must guarantee that Iraq will never again be a threat to Iran. Third, it must increase its authority within the Muslim world against Sunni Muslims, whom it regards as rivals and sometimes as threats.

Now consider the overlaps. The United States is in a war against some (not all) Sunnis. These are Iran's enemies, too. Iran does not want U.S. troops along its eastern and western borders. In point of fact, the United States does not want this either. The United States does not want any interruption of oil flow through Hormuz. Iran much prefers profiting from those flows to interrupting them. Finally, the Iranians understand that it is the United States alone that is Iran's existential threat. If Iran can solve the American problem, its regime survival is assured. The United States understands, or should, that resurrecting the Iraqi counterweight to Iran is not an option: It is either U.S. forces in Iraq or accepting Iran's unconstrained role.

Therefore, as an exercise in geopolitical theory, consider the following. Washington's current options are unacceptable. By redefining the issue in terms of dealing with the consequences of the 2003 invasion of Iraq, there are three areas of mutual interest. First, both powers have serious quarrels with Sunni Islam. Second, both powers want to see a reduction in U.S. forces in the region. Third, both countries have an interest in assuring the flow of oil, one to use the oil, the other to profit from it to increase its regional power.

The strategic problem is, of course, Iranian power in the Persian Gulf. The Chinese model is worth considering here. China issued bellicose rhetoric before and after Nixon's and [former secretary of state Henry] Kissinger's visits. But whatever it did internally, it was not a major risk-taker in its foreign policy. China's relationship with the United States was of critical importance to China. Beijing fully understood the value of this relationship, and while it might continue to rail about imperialism, it was exceedingly careful not to undermine this core interest.

From the American standpoint, an understanding with Iran would have the advantage of solving an increasingly knotty problem.

The major risk of the third strategy is that Iran will overstep its bounds and seek to occupy the oil-producing countries of the Persian Gulf. Certainly, this would be tempting, but it would bring a rapid American intervention. The United States would not block indirect Iranian influence, however, from financial participation in regional projects to more significant roles for the Shia in Arabian states. Washington's limits for Iranian power are readily defined and enforced when exceeded.

The great losers in the third strategy, of course, would be the Sunnis in the Arabian Peninsula. But Iraq aside, they are incapable of defending themselves, and the United States has no long-term interest in their economic and political relations. So long as the oil flows, and no single power directly controls the entire region, the United States does not have a stake in this issue.

Israel would also be enraged. It sees ongoing American-Iranian hostility as a given. And it wants the United States to eliminate the Iranian nuclear threat. But eliminating this threat is not an option given the risks, so the choice is a nuclear Iran outside some structured relationship with the United States or within it. The choice that Israel might want, a U.S.-Iranian conflict, is unlikely. Israel can no more drive American strategy than can Saudi Arabia.

From the American standpoint, an understanding with Iran would have the advantage of solving an increasingly knotty problem. In the long run, it would also have the advantage of being a self-containing relationship. Turkey is much more powerful than Iran and is emerging from its century-long shell. Its relations with the United States are delicate. The United States would infuriate the Turks by doing this deal, forcing them to become more active faster. They would thus emerge in Iraq as a counterbalance to Iran. But Turkey's anger at the United States would serve U.S. interests. The Iranian position in Iraq would be temporary, and the United States would not have to break its word as Turkey eventually would eliminate Iranian influence in Iraq.

Ultimately, the greatest shock of such a maneuver on both sides would be political. The U.S.-Soviet agreement shocked Americans deeply, the Soviets less so because Stalin's pact with [Adolf] Hitler had already stunned them. The Nixon-Mao entente shocked all sides. It was utterly unthinkable at the time, but once people on both sides thought about it, it was manageable.

Such a maneuver would be particularly difficult for U.S. President Barack Obama, as it would be widely interpreted as another example of weakness rather than as a ruthless and cunning move. A military strike would enhance his political standing, while an apparently cynical deal would undermine it. Ahmadinejad could sell such a deal domestically much more easily. In any event, the choices now are a nuclear Iran, extended airstrikes with all their attendant consequences, or something else. This is what something else might look like and how it would fit in with American strategic tradition.

Organizations to Contact

The editors have compiled the following list of organizations concerned with the issues debated in this book. The descriptions are derived from materials provided by the organizations. All have publications or information available for interested readers. The list was compiled on the date of publication of the present volume; the information provided here may change. Be aware that many organizations take several weeks or longer to respond to inquiries, so allow as much time as possible.

Carnegie Endowment for International Peace
1779 Massachusetts Avenue NW
Washington, DC   20036-2103
(202) 483-7600 • fax: (202) 483-1840
e-mail: info@carnegieendowment.org
Web site: www.carnegieendowment.org

The Carnegie Endowment for International Peace is a private, nonprofit organization dedicated to advancing cooperation between nations and promoting active international engagement by the United States. Founded in 1910, its work is nonpartisan and dedicated to achieving practical results. The group's Web site contains a section on Iran that provides news, official reports, links to publications, and other information about the Middle East country. Publications available include policy briefs titled "Iran Says 'No'—Now What?" "Sanctions Against Iran?" and "The Future of the Opposition and the Islamic Republic."

Council on Foreign Relations
Harold Pratt House, 58 East Sixty-eighth Street
New York, NY   10065
(212) 434-9400 • fax: (212) 434-9800
Web site: www.cfr.org

The Council on Foreign Relations (CFR) is an independent, nonpartisan membership organization, think tank, and publisher dedicated to improving understanding of U.S. foreign policy and international affairs. Headquartered in New York City, with an additional office in Washington, D.C., CFR publishes a bimonthly journal, *Foreign Affairs*, and has an extensive Web site that features reports, books, expert interviews, meeting transcripts, audios, videos, crisis guides and time lines, and press releases. A search of CFR's Web site produces a list of publications related to Iran, including "A Strategy for Iran" and "Thinking the Unthinkable: War with Iran."

Foreign Policy Research Institute

1528 Walnut Street, Suite 610, Philadelphia, PA 19102
(215) 732-3774 • fax: (215) 732-4401
e-mail: fpri@fpri.org
Web site: www.fpri.org

The Foreign Policy Research Institute (FPRI) is a nonprofit organization devoted to bringing the insights of scholarship to bear on the development of policies that advance U.S. national interests. FPRI conducts research on pressing issues, including developments in Iran and other parts of the Middle East, and publishes a quarterly journal, *Orbis*, as well as a series of bulletins and analyses. Recent publications include "The Future of Iran" and "Redefining U.S. Interests in the Middle East."

Hoover Institution—Iran Democracy Project

434 Galvez Mall, Stanford University
Stanford, CA 94305-6010
(650) 723-1754
Web site: www.hoover.org

The Hoover Institution, located at Stanford University in California, is a public policy research center devoted to advanced study of politics, economics, and political economy—both domestic and foreign—as well as international affairs. Its Iran Democracy Project was created to understand the process and prospects for democracy in Iran and the rest of the Middle East. The central goal is to help the West understand the complexities of the Muslim world and to map out possible trajectories for transitions to democracy and free markets in the Middle East, beginning with Iran. The project also seeks to identify, analyze, and offer policy options on the existing obstacles to democratic transition and to ensure that policy makers in Washington receive advice that is nonpartisan and reliable. An example of publications available on the Web site is "The Right Way to Engage Iran."

Institute for Policy Studies

1112 Sixteenth Street NW, Suite 600, Washington, DC   20036
(202) 234-9382 • fax: (202) 387-7915
e-mail: info@ips-dc.org
Web site: www.ips-dc.org

The Institute for Policy Studies (IPS) is a progressive multi-issue think tank that has served as a policy and research resource for visionary social justice movements for over four decades—from the anti-war and civil rights movements in the 1960s to the peace and global justice movements of the last decade. Seeking to influence policy makers, the press, the public, and key social movements, IPS publishes a wide variety of materials, including books, reports, op-eds, commentaries, fact sheets, talking points, speeches, and event transcripts. A search of IPS's Web site produces numerous publications on Iran and the Middle East, examples of which include "Iran Hawks Find New Supporters Against the NIE" and "Managing the Iranian Challenge."

Pars Times

e-mail: webmaster@parstimes.com

Pars Times is a nonprofit, nonpartisan, independent Web site that targets researchers, scholars, and investors. It seeks to provide comprehensive information about Iran and the Middle East by acting as a general Web guide and gateway to a variety of free resources available on the Internet. The site, especially a section titled "U.S.-Iran Relations" under the Iran tab, provides a wealth of information about Iran, including many publications detailing the modern history of Iran and offering commentary on U.S.-Iran politics.

U.S. Department of State

2201 C Street NW, Washington, DC   20520
(202) 647-4000
Web site: www.state.gov

The U.S. Department of State is a federal agency that advises the president on issues of foreign policy. Its Web site includes a section called "Countries" that provides a great deal of information about the country of Iran, including an overview of the nation and materials relating to reconstruction, U.S. aid, and the North Atlantic Treaty Organization's (NATO's) involvement in the country.

Bibliography

Books

Ervand
Abrahamian
A History of Modern Iran.
Cambridge, UK: Cambridge
University Press, 2008.

Saïd Amir
Arjomand
*After Khomeini: Iran Under His
Successors.* New York: Oxford
University Press, 2009.

Robert Baer
*The Devil We Know: Dealing with the
New Iranian Superpower.* New York:
Three Rivers Press, 2008.

Shirin Ebadi and
Azadeh Moaveni
*Iran Awakening: One Woman's
Journey to Reclaim Her Life and
Country.* New York: Random House,
2006.

Reese W. Erlich
*The Iran Agenda: The Real Story of
U.S. Policy and the Middle East Crisis.*
Sausalito, CA: PoliPointPress, 2007.

Mike Evans
*Atomic Iran: Countdown to
Armageddon . . . How the West Can
Be Saved.* Phoenix, AZ: Time Worthy
Books, 2009.

Ali Gheissari, ed.
*Contemporary Iran: Economy, Society,
Politics.* New York: Oxford University
Press, 2009.

Dore Gold
*The Rise of Nuclear Iran: How Tehran
Defies the West.* Washington, DC:
Regnery Press, 2009.

Mark Edward Harris	*Inside Iran*. San Francisco, CA: Chronicle Books, 2008.
Stephen Kinzer	*All the Shah's Men: An American Coup and the Roots of Middle East Terror*. Hoboken, NJ: John Wiley & Sons, 2008.
Hooman Majd	*The Ayatollah Begs to Differ: The Paradox of Modern Iran*. New York: Doubleday, 2008.
Roxana Saberi	*Between Two Worlds: My Life and Captivity in Iran*. New York: Harper, 2010.
Amir Taheri	*The Persian Night: Iran Under the Khomeinist Revolution*. New York: Encounter Books, 2009.
Ray Takeyh	*Guardians of the Revolution: Iran and the World in the Age of the Ayatollahs*. New York: Oxford University Press, 2009.
Ray Takeyh	*Hidden Iran: Paradox and Power in the Islamic Republic*. New York: Times Books, 2006.

Periodicals

Atlantic	"Iran in Iraq," May 2007. www.theatlantic.com.

Sharon Begley   "When Nukes Become Sacred: The Psychology Behind Iranian Support for the Country's Nuclear Program," *Newsweek*, January 8, 2010. www.newsweek.com.

John R. Bolton   "Iraq's Victory, Iran's Loss," *New York Times*, February 2, 2009. www.nytimes.com.

William Burr   "The History of Iran's Nuclear Energy Program," *Bulletin of the Atomic Scientists*, January 19, 2009. www.thebulletin.org.

Ted Galen Carpenter   "Iran's Influence in Iraq," *Sacramento Bee*, March 6, 2008.

Abbas Djavadi   "After Elections, Iran Remains a Major Player in Iraq," Radio Free Europe/Radio Liberty, March 8, 2010. www.rferl.org.

Robert Dreyfuss   "Obama's Iran Problem: Why Obama Might Bomb Iran," *Mother Jones*, January/February 2009. http://motherjones.com.

Farideh Farhi   "Iran's 'Now What' Moment," Antiwar.com, February 18, 2010. http://original.antiwar.com.

Michael Gerson   "U.S. Solidarity Could Boost Iran's Green Revolution," *Washington Post*, February 3, 2010. www.washingtonpost.com.

Jeffrey Goldberg   "Netanyahu to Obama: Stop
                    Iran—or I Will," *Atlantic*, March
                    2009. www.theatlantic.com.

Meir Javedanfar   "Tehran's Nuclear Glue: Efforts to
                   Boost Uranium Stockpiles Are Aimed
                   at Internal and External Challenges
                   to the Regime," *Guardian*, February
                   8, 2010. www.guardian.co.uk.

Flynt Leverett   "Another Iranian Revolution? Not
and Hillary   Likely," *New York Times*, January 5,
Mann Leverett   2010. www.nytimes.com.

Robert Maginnis   "Iraq Election Buys Time for
                   Democracy," *Human Events*, March
                   15, 2010. www.humanevents.com.

Ryan Mauro   "The Mullahs Make the Green
                   Revolution Invisible to the Media,"
                   Frontpagemag.com, February 12,
                   2010. http://frontpagemag.com.

Michael McFaul,   "A Win-Win U.S. Strategy for
Abbas Milani, and Dealing with Iran," *Washington
Larry Diamond   Quarterly*, Winter 2006–2007.
                   www.twq.com.

Greg Reeson   "Iraq, Iran and the New Shiite
                   Crescent," *American Chronicle*,
                   January 8, 2007.
                   www.americanchronicle.com.

Mohammed A.   "US Ambassador Accuses Iran of
Salih   Role in Iraq Election Ban,"
                   Antiwar.com, February 19, 2010.
                   http://original.antiwar.com.

Robert Wright "Listen to the Iranian People," *New York Times*, February 9, 2010. http://opinionator.blogs.nytimes.com.

Robin Wright "Iran's Opposition Loses a Mentor but Gains a Martyr," *Time*, December 21, 2009. www.time.com.

Fareed Zakaria "Containing a Nuclear Iran," *Newsweek*, October 3, 2009. www.newsweek.com.

Index

Numerals